GW00392579

All Hell and Autocross
.... more Hell and Rallycross

All Hell and Autocross
....more Hell and Rallycross

PETER CARRICK

Pelham Books

First published in Great Britain by
PELHAM BOOKS LTD
52 Bedford Square
*London, W.C.*1
1971

7207 0463 4

Set and printed in Great Britain by
Tonbridge Printers Ltd, Peach Hall Works,
Tonbridge, Kent, in Garamond eleven on thirteen point
on paper supplied by P . F. Bingham Ltd, and
bound by James Burn at Esher, Surrey

Contents

CONTENTS

Illustrations

Grateful acknowledgement is made to the following for the reproduction of the photographs indicated. Victor Marenghi and BARC 1, Bruce Stevens 2, David Thurland and BARC 3, F. Scatley 5, British Leyland 6, 7, 10, 11, 12, 13, 14, Foto-Call and Wills 8, 9.

Foreword

by MURRAY WALKER
BBC Motor Sport Commentator

Autocross and Rallycross are exciting and spectacular branches of motor sport to which an increasing number of people have been attracted in the last couple of years. While autocross remains largely an amateur or semi-professional sport, the development of rallycross with spectacular television series has brought more into competition the professional drivers and works-entered cars.

For both autocross and rallycross there is now a large and growing following and to all of us who are excited by this particular type of abandoned motoring over the rough – whether competing or watching – *All Hell and Autocross . . . More Hell and Rallycross* – is certain to make a strong appeal.

The author has produced a well documented manuscript which, while crammed with facts and information, never strays far from the special spirit and atmosphere of 'the crosses'. He captures well the vigour, the excitement and the uninhibited nature of the sport and the end result is a stimulating, vivid and absorbing book which will be read with equal zeal by the devoted enthusiast and the TV viewer alike.

Acknowledgements

I have drawn on the knowledge and experience of a great many people in the preparation of this book. To those who are mentioned and featured within the text, to those who unfortunately and because of space limitations, are not, and to the scores of individuals with whom I have had correspondence and conversations, I express my thanks.

I am also grateful to the many motor clubs who have helped me, to the organisations, official bodies, journalists, PROs, and companies both large and small for their support.

In return I can only hope that, in the publication of *All Hell and Autocross . . . More Hell and Rallycross* they will feel their effort in some measure justified.

I

The Start of it All

They contain themselves with difficulty, held back by a man with a small flag, their engines revving hysterically and collectively buzzing like a cloud of bees round a hive. Down goes the flag, the buzz becomes a roar and flesh tingles with excitement as the cluster of little cars, including always the crab-like minis, surge forward.

So explosive is that first surge of power that engines seem to race wildly ahead of the vehicles, to catch up only yards ahead as the cars shoot off the tarmac and hit the rough.

Now the battle is intense as drivers, crash-hatted and already becoming obscured by the flying mud which clings like limpets to windscreens and side panes, wrestle for control of their flying, acrobatic cars. Instinctively a foot dabs hard on the brake, then pushes back on the accelerator. Seconds are a lifetime as the clutch is pumped and drivers work with rough skill through the gears.

Just look at that! Hearts pound hard as a car ricochets high, angular and deformed-looking, all four wheels off the ground. By a miracle it seems the car regains the tarmac, crashing down hard on the suspension; and the driver thankfully stays in charge. Spectators catch up with their breathing as drivers give full lock one way, then the other, as they set up their cars for a second time round.

This is Rallycross. No excitement is quite like it. It's outrageous. It's skilful. It's messy and muddy. It's hell! To an increasingly large audience it's compulsive viewing, a kind of instant entertainment which glues their eyes to the telly and lets that mid-afternoon cuppa go cold.

Drivers become addicted, not really for the money because rallycross doesn't gross a fortune, even for the experts, but because it is what it is: a great new motor sport with a special kind of challenge. It shuns the glamour of the great Grand Prix. Nor does it provide the qualities of endurance, razor-sharp tactics and timing, and painstaking detail of a long-distance rally. It fits in neatly somewhere between, filling the gap with a dash and spirit lacking in a rally; with an astringency not found on the major race circuits of the world.

There is an instant plausibility about it all. The cars look like cars we all know: the mini next door, the Cortina down the road, the sports job seen every day in the office car park. And unlike the Formula 1 crews who exist in a privileged world of jet planes, mansions abroad and agents who promote their off-circuit image and commercial potential, rallycross drivers like Hugh Wheldon and Peter Harper seem to look and live much like you and me.

It's earthy. It has a realism likely as much to excite the chap next door as it does you. It is down-to-earth racing amid the mud, rain and dust of the English countryside. We recognise it all instantly, the entire situation, and can identify ourselves with it. Dammit, if we had the time it is something we could even have a go at ourselves...

Rallycross is merely a commercial version of autocross dreamed up by Robert Reed in the battle for television viewers, though he went a roundabout way to find it. As an early director of Independent Television's *World of Sport*, he puzzled over rallies and why they, in themselves exciting and popular, produced such dismal television. He changed things a bit, eliminated the 'non-event' sections of a rally, kept and

14

telescoped the exciting bits and, in producing a new and thrilling form of instant TV, was simply devising a spectator-orientated form of autocross which had itself developed from trials and rallies a decade before.

There is an irresistibility about thrashing a battered car around a virgin field, particularly when you can time yourself against someone else's best performance. It yields a kind of fiendish pleasure, as many competitors in trials and rallies discovered.

The trial, in which motor cyclists and later car drivers pitted their skills, strength and courage against the geography of the countryside, developed with the introduction of timed sections. These became necessary as everyone got more skilful and as a means of deciding an increasing number of ties. What wasn't fully anticipated at the time was the fun these timed sections, in themselves, would provide.

Tentatively at first, came the occasional meeting which consisted solely of these timed runs. More and more took place and it wasn't long before somebody discovered you could have even more fun if you ran a couple of cars at a time.

Autocross, in format if not in name, was on the way.

The origins of autocross are obscured by the mud and dust of those early thrashes round local fields, when nobody bothered to take down results or make any records. That great character Bert Westwood, a founder member of the British Trial and Rally Drivers' Association and regarded by many as the father of autocross, will tell you it was the old East Anglia Motor Club, now sadly defunct, which started autocross when they ran a timed event over a trials course which was very very rough and suitable only for Specials. 'It was very spectacular and very hectic,' remembers Bert. Some credit the official conception of the new sport to the Hagley and District Light Car Club, who ran an autocross of sorts in 1947 at a venue just off the Stourbridge-Bridgnorth road. Events were being held in Dorset and East Anglia in the early 1950s, but before that, perhaps in the late 1940s, it is probable that a number of these new-style burn ups were taking place by stalwarts in many parts of the country.

As we turn into the Fifties we find more closely defined records of an autocross held on Dunstable Downs by the London Motor Club and the Sporting Owner Drivers' Club of Dunstable.

Dr G. E. Pinkerton, a member of the Sporting Owner Drivers' Club in the early Fifties, recalls that it probably all started in 1952 with a letter in the magazine *Autosport* from Tony Rumfitt, at that time a well-known trials and rally driver, suggesting timed runs over a grass course. The Sporting Owner Drivers' Club at that time used to meet at the London Gliding Club on Dunstable Downs and several members, including Dr Pinkerton, were active gliding enthusiasts and enjoyed a close liaison between the gliding and motoring clubs. Reports Dr Pinkerton: 'Richmond Pike, the photographer, suggested that we should get Tony Rumfitt down and try out this new sport, using part of the gliding club's field. He duly came to lunch with us and later on we laid out an experimental course and had a jolly afternoon running a meeting for ourselves'.

Dr Pinkerton says he has a photograph somewhere of his Ulster Austin in full flight on that occasion.

It was later decided that the London Motor Club and the SODC should jointly promote a meeting early the following year, but when approached the RAC admitted to having no idea what the regulations should be, and left the organisers to devise some themselves!

The meeting was regarded as a great success. Says Dr Pinkerton: 'It was a most interesting course with marvellous spectator facilities and we had a very good entry. I recall the hairy motoring of the late "Goff" Imhoff in his redoubtable Cadillac-Allard, though I believe FTD (fastest time of the day) went to Bert Westwood in his Fiat Special.

'I was the steward for the SODC and the late Sydney Allard for LMC. He brought down a hot saloon, similar to

16

his Monte winning one, and after every few runs remarked:
"Doc – I think the stewards should inspect the course!" So
round we would go, faster and faster each time. The time-
keepers began to time us and this must be one of the rare
occasions when the actual FTD was made by the stewards!'

During the interval many of the spectating club members
were allowed to try the circuit. 'At one time,' reports Dr
Pinkerton, 'there were about fifty cars all having the most
monumental dice. Surprisingly, no one was hurt, but imagine
the RACs reaction to such happenings today'.

Indeed .. !

Early autocross meetings were all very friendly, amateur
and unscientific. Enthusiasts competed in the cars they had
driven there: and they drove them back home again, often
battered and bruised, after it was all over. There was hardly
any organisation. It was simply a rugged race round a field
borrowed from a local farmer. But the idea caught on and
autocross developed.

It was ideal for many drivers – easy and quick to organise;
easy and quick to take part in. Here was a motor sport for the
average bloke who enjoyed a quick drive but saw the traditional
racing car scene well beyond his reach, nor was attracted to
the physical fatigue and long distance tedium of rallying.

Here was a sport for amateurs run by amateurs and on this
basis autocross attracted continually growing support. Cars
competed on a short, closed circuit, usually in some convenient
field with parking facilities nearby for spectators, who at first
were mainly families and friends of the drivers. It was all
great fun and nobody bothered about keeping records. A
victory in just one event was in itself all the thrill, recognition
and reward asked for: and if you were lucky to go fastest
more than once in the afternoon you walked as tall among the
local gathering as Stirling Moss or Graham Hill ever did at
Le Mans or the Nurburgring.

By 1954 autocross was beginning to grow out of its falter-
ing beginnings and a special landmark was established on

August Bank Holiday of that year by the Taunton Motoring Club, who organised the first of a series of regular autocross events.

Car clubs in other parts of the country were also, by this time, having a go at this new-fangled fun racing, but it was the Taunton Club again, in 1959, who were granted the first permit to stage a National British Autocross event. Bill Cawsey, the club's captain and president in those days and now sadly no longer among us, was the man who fostered and pursued the idea and as a result the Taunton Motoring Club held for the following seven years what amounted to a National Championship Autocross, attracting the best drivers and machines from all over the country.

Autocross was now steady on its knees if not firmly on its feet, but for a long time it remained almost exclusively a sport for the doer and the amateur and whether anyone turned up to watch or not mattered little.

Right until the mid-Sixties it continued to be almost exclusively an amateur sport on a local level, but soon it was to become sufficiently popular to have its commercial potential noticed.

At about this time John Player & Sons, the tobacco combine, had just brought out their new coupon cigarette No. 6. Denied the promotional impact of television, for by this time cigarette advertising had been banned from TV, they were looking for alternative ways of promoting their new product and cocked a sharp ear to a suggestion from Sales Link Ltd., who had been in the motoring public relations field for some years, that they should support the new, up-and-coming sport of autocross.

Player's were thus the first firm to spot the growing potential in autocross and, through Sales Link Ltd., set up a regional pilot championship in the East Midlands in 1966. This was really the sound-out for a national series which began the following year and continued for a further three years.

Peter Watkin, from Southend, driving a Lotus Elan, holds the distinction of winning that first-ever autocross national championship sponsored by Player's No. 6. Names since added to the record books are Rod Chapman, winner for 1968, who drove various Ford Escorts and Cortinas during the season but won the championship at Silverstone in a Cortina TC borrowed from Paddy Thorne; and Mike Day, who won the title the following year in a TVR. Both Chapman and Day hail from Kent, a county which quickly began to establish a reputation for autocross drivers. The 1970 Player's No. 6 Autocross Champion was John Bevan, a 24-year-old garage proprietor from Gloucestershire, who scored an exciting victory in a home-built special.

As autocross spread its wings it attracted the semi-pro driver and while more sophisticated competition at a national level was seen to be inevitable by all but the most naïve, there continued to be an abundance of local activity to attract the enthusiastic clubman.

Robert Reed's television Rallycross finally brought this rip-roaring sport to a vast audience and it's anybody's guess just how many young drivers went out in search of their nearest autocross club after being thrilled and excited in their own armchairs by watching the experts charge round Cadwell Park or Lydden.

In under a decade autocross developed from what many people considered to be a poor man's car race, scrappily organised and poorly supported, into a major motor sport in its own right; yet in the process it happily lost none of the gutsy adventure and oily vulnerability to which its pioneers were exposed and which to them had constituted such a challenge.

The particular appeal of autocross comes through most when you see its battling at close quarters. It's a rugged, commando-type adventure where the combat is close and un-yielding, and you need to be in among it or watching from just across the way to feel the intensity of it all.

If you're driving you bounce up and down hard in your seat as you storm along the straight, whipping the car up to pinch those few extra yards that can count most of all at the end. For the tenth time you raise hell with yourself for falling back at the start because now you can't even see the bloke in front – you've lost him in the great dust cloud he's kicking up. As you hit the bend you're going great, but you'd be much happier if you weren't travelling *quite* so fast sideways. And towards the end you're battling hard to keep your car, which has become a monster, the right way up after you jumped the car ahead in a final fling to get in front.

If you're watching there's that special magic of autocross all around. The familiar looking cars in the paddock (but what unlikely sights you visualise hidden beneath the bonnet and underneath!); the overalled drivers and their modest retinue of family and fans; the screaming twin-carb engines; the cut and thrust of battle; the smell, the noise, the mud or the dust; the minis, sports jobs and those close-to-the-ground buggies and frantic-looking specials. It's all there, at all the best autocross meetings.

This is autocross with the lid off. This is the special kind of magic for anyone who thrills to the uninhibited blast of exhaust and can pin-point the skill and daring of men who race rough-shod over bumps and holes, dips and inclines, often in ordinary-looking cars, in all kinds of weather conditions.

It has a gritty kind of vigour which fits in well with the brash, persistent energy of the internal combustion engine going at full cog. It is all this which spells adventure and excitement for thousands, both driving and watching.

2

Autocross Today

Such is the impact of autocross today that no matter where you live you are likely to find club events taking place at some time or other within just a few miles of your own front door.

The RAC calendar of events has listed around 450 autocrosses each year since 1967, when the tally shot up to 493, from 349 the previous year. As the majority of events are held during the recognised autocross season between March and October – and it is essentially a weekend sport taking place mainly on Sunday – it is not difficult to work out that a large number of drivers each weekend are caught up in the fun, speed and excitement of this thing called autocross. It is now a major club sport where speed events are concerned.

Its origins were modest, its early events unencumbered by rules and restrictions on who could take part, and it remains today perhaps the most democratic of all motor sports, attracting people of all kinds from virtually every social and economic background. While for the major national events the fans now turn out in force – and the proportion of females present is likely to surprise and delight the first-time male attender! – it is still at a local level essentially a *competing* sport, though the numbers who watch autocrosses have increased steadily over the years – 2,000–3,000 at well attended local events, 8,000–10,000 at a Final, now by no means uncommon.

Cars reflect the democratic nature of autocross. Some carry modifications no more elaborate than protective metal plates to prevent damage from grounding, while the more sophisticated national-competing cars, often part-sponsored entries, carry extras costing £1,000 and more. The thrill is all the greater when, as sometimes happens still, a brash young pup with little experience and a virtually standard model, has the cheek to enter and against more expensive cars and more experienced drivers, somehow manages to win : though the chances, to be admitted, become more slim as competition becomes fiercer and standards rise.

In the tearaway early days of autocross nobody bothered with classes and the smooth, shiny saloon of recent vintage came naturally into competition with a dull old banger. Whatever you had was tuned to the best of your ability and to the extent of your pocket, and left to fight it out against all-comers. Uneven though the matching may have appeared, the rigours and demands of the natural course had its own methods of evening out the odds . . . and producing some amazing and startling results.

Today autocross has a more ordered way of going on. Cars are grouped in classes to make competition keener but the cut and thrust of the past remains in the atmosphere of a national meeting as the fastest cars on the day, irrespective of class, come together in the glorious, all-glorifying knock out to decide the outright winner.

And it's all more specialised now. The traditional rally car to which a driver would at one time make few if any modifications as a concession to his autocrossing, is seen far less. It's too weighty and it is now being lined up against an increasing number of cars which have been specially prepared for autocross – plenty of race performance in the engine, enough low-speed traction to see you through wet conditions, and bodywork cut to the minimum to eliminate weight you don't need.

It may look grotty and stark, but increasingly it has been

prepared for the one job it has to do; and autocross cars are now often towed carefully to the meeting on a special-purpose trailer. Whatever happened to those early 'anything goes' days!

Cars generally compete two together, screaming away from the start line side by side, racing to be ahead into that first, important bend; but the two-at-a-time start is not set down in the basic rules as a necessity. Because of the limitations of certain courses, autocross cars sometimes set off singly, though from a spectating point of view some of the spectacle is lost; while the Barley Mo event, and several clubs mainly in Devon, have gained a reputation for 'four abreast' starts.

Officially the course must be not less than 600 yards long and 30 feet wide before cars can be set off in pairs simultaneously. Once the slower of the first two cars has travelled at least 300 yards from the start line, a second pair can be flagged away. Where the course is wider and longer – not less than 40 feet wide and 1,200 yards long – a third pair of cars can be started when the slower of the second pair is at least 200 yards from the start line. This means that six cars can be racing round the course at the same time, providing plenty of excitement for the fans.

Even on smaller courses where two cars are not permitted to be started simultaneously, provision has been made to avoid what could soon develop into a rather pedestrian procession of single cars going round the course. So if the course is less than 30 feet wide, the second car can be flagged away once the first car has travelled one-third of a lap or 200 yards, whichever is the lesser. And on a longish course, not less than 600 yards, three cars can be in competition consecutively, starting off at 200 yard intervals.

There are now eight class events listed in the RAC's *Motor Sport Year Book* – known as the Blue Book. These are:

1. Front wheel drive saloons up to 1000 cc.
2. Sports and GT cars up to 1300 cc. (rear wheel drive).
3. Rear wheel drive, front engine saloons up to 1300 cc.

23

4. Specials, derivatives and other vehicles not eligible for any other class.
5. Front wheel drive saloons over 1000 cc.
6. Sports and GT cars over 1300 cc. (rear wheel drive).
7. Rear engined, rear wheel drive saloons, all capacities.
8. Rear wheel drive, front engined saloons over 1300 cc.

These, and the other regulations which govern autocross, are stipulated by the RAC, who now control all autocrosses held in England, Wales, Scotland and Northern Ireland. Their definition of the sport is simple and to the point: *A race or speed event on a grass or unsealed surface.*

Many of the regulations are safety measures drafted in the interest of competitor and spectator alike: drivers must wear suitable clothing and an approved crash helmet; practice runs have to be made in conditions similar to those expected in the competition; drivers aren't allowed to smoke during the event – as if there was time! A minimum distance must be maintained between the course and the spectators and between the course and the paddock – 100 feet where there is no barrier designed to halt a competing car between these enclosures and the course, or, where there is a barrier, not less than 75 feet all the way round corners and 60 feet along the straights. The minimum acceptable barrier is two rows of straw bales or equivalent, placed approximately half-way between the course and the enclosures. The rows of bales must be approximately ten feet apart and if each row is not continuous, any gaps must not exceed the length of a bale.

The regulations also insist upon fire equipment being available at all danger points and a minimum of one doctor, ambulance and crew, in attendance.

Autocross drivers sometimes have harsh comments to make on the list of rules which now govern autocross, and the RAC, like all official bodies, is sometimes subjected to criticism. The unfettered nature of autocross in which we see ordinary-looking cars having an all-out thrash around a rough

field is what appeals most and drivers are right in their fear
that too many rules and regulations would kill the enjoyment.
At the same time drivers will tell you that autocross isn't
dangerous. If this is so, it is probably because rules have been
kept to a minimum and have not been allowed to impose too
harshly on the undisciplined nature of the sport, which is the
basic delight of autocross.

Once the flag drops the driver doesn't have too many rules
to worry about. He has to keep his car on course because if he
gets all four wheels off he is immediately eliminated (and
what fantastic driving we sometimes see *off* the course!) and
he must avoid taking markers along with him because according to the RAC rules each marker down carries a five seconds
penalty.

Other than that, plus driving with great skill and daring
and in conditions which are best when they are just about as
bad as you can get them, the autocross ace has little to worry
about!

Drivers are an assorted bunch and although increasingly you
come across the specialist who has restricted almost all his
racing to autocross, there are plenty of chaps who took to the
sport after riding motor cycles in scrambles and trials, and plenty
of others who are also rally drivers and even racing drivers.

The great thing about autocross is its special brand of all-
the-way action and excitement and it's not surprising that it
has become so popular so quickly. It gives excellent value for
money to everyone taking part, driving or watching. Con-
testants can show off their driving skills and daring at modest
cost, while spectators are always close enough to the action to
get a good view of what is going on. They are part of it all,
almost as much as the chaps behind the wheel.

Weather can hold the trump card in the see-sawing game of
autocross. In the mud a driver needs one particular technique
to see him through, not to mention a vehicle specially prepared
to better the conditions. When it's dry and dusty, he's got to
vary his driving and his car needs different preparation.

25

And all the time there seems to be the chance of the unusual happening: and even if it doesn't the constant high-flying action has eliminated any possibility of disappointment. When it does, the bonus comes at no extra charge.

What sort of thing? A car ending up on its roof, an extreme result from what appeared to be a perfectly normal (for auto-cross) bit of jockeying; a result reversed because the first chap across the line was judged to have jumped the start; the re-routing of the course during the meeting because of deep ruts forming; a really classic scrap between two known pro-tagonists; the unexpected disqualification; the car that un-accountably 'dies' and the chap whose driving technique is limited but nonetheless keeps his foot hard down and has the crowd stretching; the innocent-looking shunt which sends the mini cartwheeling.

Sooner or later it's all there in autocross – plus a post-ponement because of foot-and-mouth! – yes, it actually did happen.

If you're watching autocross for the first time you'll be surprised and impressed by the speeds. Minis average in the region of 40 mph, while 50–60 mph is not unusual in the faster classes. Not much perhaps, when compared with the gleaming thoroughbreds of the Grand Prix, but over the often stony or muddy or dusty, and always punishingly uneven ground, it really is flying.

Because of their phenomenal success, Minis of one sort or another – and specifically Mini-Coopers – have become synonymous with autocross in the public eye, but one of the fascinations of present day events is the wide variety of cars competing.

Taking the entries for the 1970 Autocross Championship sponsored by Players as a fair example of the scope of this variety, we find Class 1 (front wheel drive saloons up to 1000 cc.) and Class 5 (front wheel drive saloons over 1000 cc.) dominated by the Mini Cooper, the Mini Cooper S, of course, in the latter category.

In Class 2, however, for sports and GT cars up to 1300 cc. (rear wheel drive), the entries were more varied, bringing in the Austin Healey Sprite, a couple of specials, an MG Midget and a Triumph Herald. Anglias and Escorts made up the majority of entries in the rear wheel drive, front-engined section for saloons up to 1300 cc., though snuggling between we find a Fiat 124, a Morris Minor and even an Austin A35!

Capturing some of the greatest attention was the class for Specials, Derivatives and Other Vehicles and hardly any wonder. Just look what the list included: Flymo 1275 cc.; Groundhog Special; Tiger Twin; a VW Beach Buggy; and the Cannonball-Whistani!

Sprites faced competition from the 3800 cc. E-types in the Sports and GT Class (over 1300 cc.) rear wheeled drive category, and also from TVR Vixens, MGBs, Lotus Elan and Triumph 1991 cc.

In the category for rear-engined, rear-wheeled drive saloons, all capacities, Imps competed alongside VWs, Renault against Sunbeam, a Porsche and a Singer Chamois, while Escorts dominated the 1300 cc. rear wheeled drive, front engined saloon category, with a Volvo and a couple of Lotus Cortinas in for good measure.

For a time the RAC ignored autocross. Perhaps they couldn't decide whether this upstart of a motor sport was a serious activity or nothing more, after all, than a crazy, seven-day wonder. Their official stamp of recognition came in 1965, and their Blue Book now makes innumerable references to autocross and officially designates it as a speed event.

Autocross events, insist the RAC, are now subject to the same general requirements as other speed events.

Hundreds of motor clubs are now running autocross events every year, from small clubs with hardly more than a handful of members and one autocross a year, to professionally organised clubs like the British Automobile Racing Club with a vast membership. The BARC, with its nationwide structure divided into sections covering London, North Thames, North

West, South East, South West, West Midlands and Yorkshire, ran as many as twelve separate autocross during the 1970–71 season. Their splendid autocross festivals are gala affairs spread over two days. The British Trials and Rally Drivers' Association is also very autocross active with their national events which start about May and go on right through the season, culminating in a well organised Final at which more than 100 drivers compete.

It was the BTRDA who organised the first autocross championship with competitors scoring points according to their class position in a series of events held throughout the season. Thus all classes of car had equal chance of winning, not necessarily the car which did the greatest number or fastest times on the day (FTDs).

The BTRDA final in 1970 produced some excellent driving with the top honours going to Brian Moorcroft in his Tony Blore Racing Midget. Runner-up was Sid Davey (Escort 1600), and other trophy winners were David Barsby, Graham Bush and Judith Jesty, all in Minis. Class winners were Brian Toogood, Gordon Howie, Tony Merridale, Harry Dickinson, Nick Jesty, David Hanchet, Mike Ranger, Ray Smith and Paul de Luca. Colin Hargreaves, the 1969 BTRDA Autocross Champion, took FTD.

But whether a very local event or a national championship meeting, the energy and enthusiasm is the same and the competition as fierce and as close in the former as in the more glamorous and highly publicised events.

Driving and speed apart, the two great hazards facing autocross drivers are mud and dust. A high degree of skill is required to keep a car going well and in the right direction, with mud inches thick sliding all four wheels and slithering the car in all directions. On dry days dust can be an even greater danger with visibility down to a few feet, giving the second man no sight of the chap up front. How do you overtake safely in such conditions? Once behind the wheel of an autocross car you quickly find out!

The autocross driver must also be on the alert for changing ground conditions which can affect his driving and the way his vehicle behaves and responds. As the meeting progresses deep grooves can develop in the subsoil, forming an additional hazard. While mud and wet can add to the spectacle and fun of autocross, too much can endanger the afternoon's entertainment, and many an organiser has bitten his nails well down to the roots as rain has threatened to bog down the cars and force an abandonment of the entire event.

A field is generally in a sorry state by the end of an autocross meeting and for this reason few permanent circuits have been established. Even when the general venue remains, the course is switched around and while this adds variety and stimulation for the drivers, it gives a gipsy-like image to the sport and tends to perpetuate its unsophistication and unprofessionalism. There is no permanent focal point, no setting up of grandstands and lavish circuit facilities, as might be envisaged with the basis of a permanent home.

John Player and Sons, the tobacco people, once they became interested in autocross commercially, began to provide portable grandstands and other facilities in an attempt to cultivate the spectator and round off the harsh corners, but such 'civilisations' could only exist at the important meetings and for the most part autocross continued to demand of its followers a kind of uncompromising devotion which rendered them impervious to extremes of sun, rain, cold, wind and even snow and sleet – not to mention the cow-dung underfoot and the dust and dirt in the face and hair.

It was sad news indeed when, just before the National Autocross Championship Final of 1970 which they were sponsoring, Players announced that following the Championship they would be withdrawing their support of autocross.

Players made no official statement, but Sales Link Press Officer, Richard Feast, said it was felt that the sport had progressed sufficiently for it to continue without further assistance from Players. Several other championships had been established since the first Player's No. 6 Championship and Players felt their money could be channelled in other, equally deserving ways.

Players, through their sponsorship, had done much to advance autocross and to lift it out of its 'backyard' environment. In the four years of their involvement autocross as a result increased its status as a fashionable sport and while it can be justifiably argued that from Player's point of view it was a sound commercial proposition, there is no doubt that autocross benefited immeasurably from their participation. The Player's No. 6 dolly girls with their shiny high boots and even higher hemlines brought with them a trendier image. So did the special exhibition drives undertaken by popular DJs, as an added attraction at the main meetings.

The purist is entitled to ask what these novelties are to do with autocross, and perhaps more important, to what depth of professionalism they would lead! But they did have the effect of drawing attention to the sport, attracting additional support and lightening an atmosphere which until then had tended to look grey, oil-stained and perhaps just a little grisly to the outside world.

As Mr J. P. Shaw, the Promotions Manager of John Player and Sons remarked: 'Ever since 1966 we have been helping to promote the sport of autocross, to make it more attractive to spectators, more rewarding for competitors and more lucrative for the clubs who run the championship so well. We are happy to be associated with the improvements that have taken place in one of the most exciting open-air sports still available to the amateur'.

The rules for that first Player's-sponsored National Autocross Championship in 1967 were not too dissimilar from the framework of what was to be the final one, in 1970, at Peterborough. The basis of the 1970 Competition was a series of preliminary events which started six months earlier. There were twenty qualifying rounds, prior to the National Final, and a competing driver could score points only in the area qualifying event which he had earlier nominated. Points in the qualifying rounds were awarded on the following basis: 1st in class – 9; 2nd in class – 6; 3rd in class – 4; 4th in class – 3; 5th in class – 2; 6th in class – 1.

Each competitor had two timed runs. Their times were added together to determine the top four positions, the lower the aggregate time, of course, the better the performance. The four leading competitors in each class then took part in a paired knock-out competition, the first and third fastest, and the second and fourth fastest being paired together. The two winners then competed against each other to determine the class winner – the two losers also competing against each other to decide 3rd and 4th places in the class. The eight class winners then competed against each other on a knock-out basis to decide the outright winner of the day. Pairing in the first runs of the knockout were according to classes and were determined by a draw conducted by the Clerk of the Course between the finish of the practice and the start of the competitive runs.

Four years earlier the first Player's-sponsored championship incorporated 32 qualifying rounds, four area semi-finals and a final at High Wycombe which attracted a crowd of 5,000, in spite of very wet conditions, to see many of the country's top competitors. Players are said to have given £6,500 in prize money alone to that first championship series, and were to go on during the next four years to spend a great deal more in their sponsorship of autocross. Their 'big event' finals were soon to become a highspot in a crowded autocross season.

At Silverstone a year later there were the same number of competitors, 136, and three times the number of people watching, 15,000, in the second championship final sponsored by Players; a similar capacity crowd thronged the grounds of ancient Woburn Abbey in 1969 to witness Mike Day drive his TVR Tuscan through the dust to become the new Player's No. 6 National Autocross Champion.

The 1970 National Final took place on a well laid out

course at Alwalton, near Peterborough, on September 20th, but the battle for places at the final had started way back in April with the first preliminary heat held by the Sevenoaks and District Motor Club. The country was divided into four geographical areas and altogether about 550 registered competitors took part in the series.

And so to the final itself, broached in an air of gloom because of Player's announcement only a few days before that they would afterwards withdraw their sponsorship of autocross. But depression was quickly dispelled by the afternoon's sunshine, the exciting racing and the carefree atmosphere of this major autocross meeting. From all over the country came top autocross drivers and the event was seen by a crowd of well over 6,000.

All the trappings and trimmings of a really big meeting were in evidence: the Player's No. 6 girls, smiling and attractive in the sun; the well attended press caravan; the bar and off-course displays; the buzz of intense activity in the paddock; the autocross fanatic, quiet but deeply knowledgeable about the cars and their modifications, the drivers, timings, conditions; the chap who hardly knew an exhaust from a plug but who, with his wife and kids in tow, was out to have a good Sunday afternoon's entertainment... all this and more was present to add to the character and the festive nature of the occasion.

All competitors in the Player's No. 6 National Championship had collected points from their four best scoring appearances, to qualify for the Final. In the Final the method of scoring was the same as in the preliminary rounds – on the basis of each driver making two timed runs, the fastest four then competing in an eliminator contest to decide their place order.

Rules for the Final also allowed a maximum of sixteen (plus two reserves) competitors in each class, these sixteen to be made up of invited class winners from Scotland and Ireland and, subject to their attendance, either the 14, 15 or 16

Whoops a Daisy! A new venue for a BARC event at Ruislip turned out to be a bit too bumpy for Mini driver J. M. Glenister of Cheshunt motor club, who neatly completed a triple roll and escaped with a severe shaking

Flying low. Richard Wharton and the Escort

M. S. Moorhead gets it all on one side as he goes on to win at a Surrey
Centre Autocross

highest placed competitors from England and Wales.

John Bevan gave notice of intent on his first run, with the twin-cam Naveb Special going really fast, but it was the Minis up to 1½ litres which opened the full and fast-moving programme. Dave Conway in a Mini backed by *Auto Race and Rally Magazine* and Brian Jones in his good-looking Beco Mini did well here, with Mike Hill and John Thurston coming up with good second runs. Brian Jones led the class with excellent timings of 1 minute 14.69 seconds and 1 minute 16.53 seconds. The class eliminators brought defeat for Thurston against some good driving by Hill while Conway, after having bent a con-rod in his own car, took over the Dave May–Bob Lamb Cooper S, but bad luck dogged him and victory went to Brian Jones. Conway moved off the faster as the flag dropped and was holding a convincing lead by the first bend. Shortly after, a burst tyre, resulting in the seat mountings shearing, put Conway out of the running after a brush with the Mick Jones Mini.

Jones faced Hill for the division award, the latter using his Cadwell rallycross experience well. He got away first and kept in front to win through.

In the class for under 1300 cc. sports and GT cars, Dave Dawson in his 1293 cc. Mk 1 Sprite had two runs in the region of 1 minute 15 seconds. Gordon Howie, who had been over eight seconds behind on time, down in 4th place, nonetheless won the class because Dave, going well in the eliminator against the Second City Midget of Howie, rolled his open Sprite in a final battle, though was unhurt.

Of the conventional 1300 cc. Saloons, Ian Semple in the cross flow 1300 GT-powered Anglia was fastest to begin with, but in the knock-out class runs Richard Wharton, who had earlier been three seconds slower than Ian, left Semple on the line and kept the advantage.

Third place was taken by Roger Lewis in an Anglia, again with cross flow power, and in fourth position was the Escort driven by Tim Stevens.

B

There was plenty of excitement and action in the Specials class, with John Bevan raising everybody's pulse rate with some thrilling motoring in the 1 minute 7 seconds bracket, including his second FTD. Bevan's remarkable 2 minutes 14.91 seconds aggregate total was almost 14 seconds better than the Tiger Twin of Derek Hearn.

Two major disappointments here: (1) the lack of challenge from Colin Hargreaves, who never got his famous Flymo started on the runs because of diff trouble; (2) that power-house V6 Cannonball-Whistarni of Howard Parkin blew a clutch after taking second BTD on the first runs, therein eliminating a challenge to John Bevan which many Parkin fans felt might well develop. So it was Bevan in the Naveb, Derek Hearn in the Tiger Twin, Richard Judge in a supercharged front-engined RJS, Stewart Stockdale in a 1108 cc. Renault Special – in that order.

Class 5 brought on the big capacity Minis and after quite a battle involving a number of drivers Gary Streat took final honours, bettering on the way the performances of Ian Cornwell and Trevor Olds. Earlier Nick Jesty had done well with an aggregate of 2 minutes 21.72 seconds, before bodging up his start against Trevor Olds in the knock-out for class awards. In spite of this mishap Nick recovered well to provide some of the closest racing of the afternoon against Trevor, who finished just ahead. Nick was credited with second place, however, and Trevor, who must have incurred a penalty, finished third.

In the class for over 1300 cc. Sports and GT cars we saw some exciting stuff from Gerald Solkow (TVR Vixen), Ron Easton (TVR Vixen), Ted Cooke (Austin Healey Sprite) and Robbie McFall (E-type Jaguar). Cooke had a great battle with McFall before the sliding E-type hedged the Sprite up and over. Ron advanced to finish only a car's length behind the racing TVR of Gerald Solkow, who won the class.

In Class 7 (rear-engined, rear wheeled drive saloons, all capacities) we saw a lot of Griff Griffiths; Bob Piper in the

Corsair 1.9-litre engined VW, Reg Hanson and Mike Ranger. Mike, on his final run in the Hillman Californian, bumped Laurie Manifold, and then again got involved with Reg Hanson in the Imp, the latter somewhat surprisingly beating Ranger before the Imp engine petered while trailing Bob Piper in their class deciding contest. Griff Griffiths took third position.

The final class for rear-wheel drive, front-engined saloons over 1300 cc., produced some spirited dicing, with Roy Owen flipping his Lotus Cortina while driving hard against the pushrod Ford Cortina of Roger Swaffer. Roy was not injured. In the eliminators Scotland's Andrew Smith, in an Escort TC, took on the Volvo 123S of Colin Grewer and came out on top, with Grewer finally occupying second place and Roger Swaffer, third.

These, then, were the class winners:
1. Mike Hill (Mini Cooper S)
2. Gordon Howie (MG Midget)
3. Richard Wharton (Ford Escort GT)
4. John Bevan (Naveb Special)
5. Gary Streat (Mini Cooper S)
6. Gerald Solkow (TVR Vixen – MGB)
7. Bob Piper (VW Saloon)
8. Andrew Smith (Ford Escort TC)

Now came the final championship knock-out, with the winners of classes 8 and 7 together, 3 and 6, 2 and 1 and 4 and 5. This brought Andrew Smith and Bob Piper in competition, Piper going through, and Richard Wharton and Gerald Solkow, Gerald just scraping home. Howie, surprisingly, in the Second City Midget, had the measure of Mike Hill, while poor Gary Streat didn't really have a chance against the all-conquering John Bevan.

Down to the final four now, with Solkow up against Bevan and Piper alongside Howie. Not unexpectedly, we saw Bevan and Piper in the final and again, not unexpectedly by this time, John and the Naveb went incredibly to give Bob no chance.

The whole affair, including good RAC organisation, sunny weather and some fiercely fought runs which produced plenty of excitement for the large crowd, was a fitting swan-song for Players in their four-year-long association with autocross. The course was good and had been planned to produce evenly-matched racing, but unfortunately the event clashed with another major autocross event. This, plus the non-arrival of all except one competitor due from Northern Ireland, meant there were 40 non-starters out of the 141 competitors listed in the programme. But those in attendance gave good money's worth and no one can have been disappointed.

An added attraction was the appearance of Radio 1 DJs Ed Stewart and Dave Lee Travers. 'Stewpot' drove the FTW47H (a World Cup rebuilt car), and Dave Lee a 1.6 litre GP Buggy. On the first run 'Stewpot' was well out of the running, but did better in a much more exciting combat later in the afternoon after Dave Lee Travers had switched to a Triple C Escort 1300 GT.

This 1970 Final consolidated the 'anything can happen' character of the sport. The electronic timing gear, donated to the RAC by Shell and used for the first time in The National Autocross Championship, repeatedly failed to produce readings when two cars crossed the line almost as one, and this necessitated quite a number of re-runs. And the starting, by flag and not lights, produced a number of exclusions because of alleged jumped starts.

But that's autocross for you . . .

3

Rallycross: A Hit on TV

A slick, fast-moving, pre-packaged version of autocross, manufactured and marketed specially for the small screen: that's rallycross. When Robert Reed created his show-stopping brainchild for Independent Television in late 1966, running his first televised meeting in January, 1967, he visibly dented the BBC's smug and acknowledged authority in the world of television sport. The extent to which 'auntie' had been scooped was only fully appreciated later, when it was revealed that ITV was collecting six million viewers for every rallycross meeting: and when in February, 1970 ITV let rallycross temporarily lapse before starting up again in November, the BBC had long since seen the potential and stepped in with a rallycross programme of their own. In 1970–71 the BBC's coverage was greater than that of Independent Television – six meetings against four, 3 hours against 1½.

Rallycross first came to life on the TV screen, but so enthusiastic did drivers become for this new-style motoring that rallycross club events are now held in many parts of the country in addition to the big-time stuff you see on television with the top drivers hurtling their works-prepared and works-assisted cars round Lydden, Croft and Cadwell Park.

Autocross and rallycross are really very much the same thing. Two major differences are the character of the course and the

37

method of starting. In rallycross drivers hurtle and slide their cars over a deliberately varied terrain of grass, tarmac and mud, with humps and inclines included to put even the best cars to severe test. The official RAC definition of rallycross reads: 'A race or speed event which takes place on a combination of a sealed and unsealed surface as part of a permanent circuit'. And rallycross cars always start four abreast, to give added spectacle for the purposes of TV.

There are even fewer rules than in autocross and once the cars line up at the start it is very much every man for himself.

There are no categories as in autocross, though in the Wills/BBC series 1970–71 4-wheel drive cars, which really meant the works Ford Capris, carried a penalty, being held back at the start for five seconds after the other cars had got away. There was no such penalty in the Castrol/ITV series – the '4-wheelers' in with an equal chance from the start.

Full marks to Robert Reed for putting on his thinking cap following the televising of a three-mile stage of the 1966 RAC Rally from Camberley, in Surrey. He came up with the plain truth that rallies could never be really big box-office TV because cars were soon lost from view; the snatches which the camera *could* show meant very little to the average viewer; the whole thing was too involved for a mass audience, what with starting points and classes, with no one being able to tell who had won until long after it was all over.

Reed said at the time: 'What we've got to do is to keep the cars in vision nearly all the time, dispense with all this nonsense of classes which only one person in 100 understands, and produce an event where the first car over the line in a matter of minutes actually wins'.

So this simplified rallying became rallycross and in a matter of weeks the first event took place at Lydden, near Canterbury. Inside a month rallycross was clearly seen as a television winner. After only six months the RAC were incorporating official rules in their renowned Blue Book. By October 1969 John Sprinzel, writing in *TV Times*, revealed that 100 rallycross drivers in Britain were competing on three tracks, each one mile long and made up of tarmac, loose gravel, grass and hazards like the yump (simulated hump back bridge) and the water splash. The BBC jumped on the bandwagon with excellent, enthusiastic commentaries from Murray Walker.

Rallycross had really arrived with 10 million viewers for the 1969 Wills Final.

Viewers found this new Saturday afternoon sport compulsive television and commonsense measures adopted by drivers, such as cutting out an aperture from the windscreen (called the letterbox look!), so *that* small area at least couldn't be covered in mud shutting out completely the driver's vision, was accepted as all part of the showmanship of this new, man-sized sport. Good camera work caught cars in flight, drivers in close-up fighting for control of their cars, the slithers, the slides and, of course, the occasional spectacular shunt.

Cars caked in thick mud; peek-a-boo holes cut in wind-screens and ingeniously constructed windscreen shades to assist vision through the flying mud; even no windscreen at all! It was all there to add to the fun and flavour of rallycross and to see the winners first to the finishing line.

Names unknown to the general viewing public became matinee idols, if not overnight, then in a very short time: Hugh Wheldon, John Rhodes, Gerry Braithwaite, Peter Harper, 'Jumping' Jeff Williamson and others. Harper virtually retired from top-flight world rallying in his excitement for the new sport and in terms of television performances quickly became one of the best known and certainly one of the most successful drivers.

In his first year of rallycross Harper initially tied for first place in the Championship, but in spite of winning four events out of the six forfeited the title on a slower time on the final day. The following year Peter Harper won outright in a glorious and breath-taking neck-and-neck finish to the *World of Sport* Championship. At the beginning of the sixth and final round at Croft only two points separated Harper,

39

in the lead, from John Rhodes, with Gerald Braithwaite, John Boulder and Pip Carrotte close behind. With the mud and stones flying in a supreme test of driving skill and nerve, Harper and Rhodes battled out the all-action final, with Peter finally coming out on top. But in 1969–70, Harper had to be content with second place to Hugh Wheldon.

Wheldon proved how important was consistently good driving in the battle for this championship. He didn't win one single round, but scored sufficiently high points throughout to put him ahead of the field – four points ahead of Peter Harper and a further nine points ahead of Barry Lee.

The free-for-all world of rallycross, as autocross, puts the works supported drivers in open competition with private entries; and not the least of its attractions is that the underdog sometimes wins. Wheldon, as a private owner driving a Mini-Cooper, usurped stout opposition from Harper (Imp), who receives some help from the motor and motor supplies manufacturers, and Lee in a works financed and works supported Ford Escort Twin Cam, to win the championship. A creditable performance indeed.

Not surprisingly, regional rallycross took root quickly, fired by the impact of television, and the series of events organised by the South Eastern Centre of the British Automobile Racing Club and sponsored by the *Kent Messenger* during 1970 was well subscribed and enthusiastically supported.

Three meetings took place at Lydden on Easter Monday, Whit Monday and August Monday, with a driver's best two performances counting to the overall Championship. The *Kent Messenger* trophy, plus a cash award of £100, was awarded to the overall champion, with £50 going to the second place winner overall, and £25 for the driver finishing in third place overall. Further awards of £20, (1st); £15 (2nd); £10 (3rd) and £5 were made for the best overall performances plus £10 for the fastest individual time in each of the three runs at each meeting.

Hugh Wheldon, by now well recognised as a phenomenal rallycross driver, was first in his exceptionally mobile and nimble 1300 cc. Austin Cooper S, with Rod Chapman second, driving a 1600 cc. Ford Escort TC, and Graham Craker (1293 cc. BMC Cooper S) in third place. A crowd of about 10,000 turned up at each meeting.

Beginning October, 1970 the famous Thames Estuary Automobile Club (TEAC) organised a new series of National British Events at Lydden, sponsored by W. D. and H. O. Wills, six meetings altogether running through until March, 1971 with all events enjoying big coverage on BBC TV Grandstand. With 58 names down on the list of entries for the first meeting on October 17th, rallycross had certainly travelled a long way as a *competitive sport* and not just as a television spectacular since Robert Reed first mentioned his idea to his boss John Bromley, Barrie Gill, then a motoring correspondent, and John Sprinzel, a rally driver, commentator and motoring journalist; and from which it all stemmed.

Even greater was the list of entries for the non-televised closed meeting on the Sunday following – no fewer than 89 drivers, including reserves, listed.

Both Saturday and Sunday events were part of Wills' ambitious rallycross programme for 1970–71, which comprised two separate championships – the W. D. and H. O. Wills Rallycross Championship 1970–71, having as qualifying rounds six Saturday meetings, and the Embassy Rallycross Trophy, having as qualifying rounds the Sunday meetings from October to February. Being closed events, the Sunday meetings were, of course, only open to members of the Thames Estuary Automobile Club, who organised both competitions.

A number of changes were made for this new series and included the following:

1. The positions at all meetings to be decided on the basis of the fastest individual run, rather than the aggregate of three runs as in the past. Championship points to be

41

allocated on this basis. Awards to be made also, however, for the best aggregate times.

2. No classes in any event.
3. Only one driver accepted for a car at all events.
4. 4-wheel drive cars to be accepted subject to a five second penalty, and these cars to start five seconds behind the other cars in their group.
5. All the Sunday events to be run under Closed permits, i.e. open only to TEAC members.
6. Medical certificates required by all drivers.

Points were awarded for overall position in each event on the following basis:

1st	10 points	6th	5 points
2nd	9 points	7th	4 points
3rd	8 points	8th	3 points
4th	7 points	9th	2 points
5th	6 points	10th	1 point

The aggregate of points scored from all the qualifying rounds counted towards the championship.

Drivers dead-heating for a place each received the full points for that place and, to make life especially exciting, double points were scored at the final qualifying round.

An additional box-office attraction for 1970–71 was an Embassy Ladies' Invitation Trophy competition, consisting of four heats, two semi-finals and a final. All events were tele-recorded by the BBC before the start of the Championship events for showing at a convenient time during 'Grandstand'. Heats consisted of one run of three laps, the fastest two drivers qualifying for the semi-finals. The fastest two drivers in each of the semi-finals then advanced to the final on March 6th.

With many drivers taking part in both the Saturday and Sunday meetings, Lydden on Rallycross week-ends took on a pronounced motor sport flavour and 'Saturday night at the Chaucer' – the Chaucer being the local hostelry – became a feature. So much a part of rallycross had the Chaucer become that TEAC urged: 'If you wish to join the party you are advised to book early as the hotel is invariably full throughout the season. Mention Rallycross when booking to take advantage of the special terms'.

With the Wills/BBC/Lydden Championship away to a flying start in October, Independent Television's coverage of the sport didn't begin until a month later, with the first of four championship rounds held at Cadwell Park, sponsored by Castrol and organised by the Lincoln Motor Cycle and Car Club with the Cadwell Car and Cart Club. Top drivers like Hugh Wheldon, Peter Harper and others started a busy season, competing in both the major televised competitions.

Important non-televised rallycross during 1970–71 included a well-paid Sunday series at Croft sponsored by Guards and with organisation by the Darlington and District Car Club. Of National British Status, there were four meetings, three heats and a Final, between November 8th and February 21st. Works and works-sponsored drivers competed in one category, Clubmen in the other and the championship resulted, reported Croft, from the enormous popularity of the Guards Clubman's Rallycross series held early in 1970. Although not qualifying for the Championship, Croft also staged a Guards Rallycross meeting on Sunday, December 27th.

Altogether an extremely active rallycross season.

At all levels rallycross provides a refreshing air of spontaneity. When the flag drops or the starting light shows you never quite know what will happen – and you don't have to wait for hours to find out. Within seconds you've pitch-forked into the thick of the action – driving or watching – and in minutes its all over. There's a pause, then the excitement is on again, as intense as before, as the next cars wait to go, snapping at the starting line.

Adding to the overall excitement and tension is the closeness of the racing. Cars are often equally matched and you need your head examining if you think you can predict rallycross winners with any degree of assurance or regularity. This maintains interest all through because seldom do you get the same car winning as a matter of course: except when miracle men like Wheldon and Harper are in the saddle.

Peter Harper, who should know about these things, believes more driving skill is required in rallycross than in rallying. 'In rallycross you have to get on to your limit quickly and stay on it. Margins are close and your judgement and skill have to be precise. There's no room for error'.

The rewards for even the top rallycross drivers are negligible, especially when set against the time and expense in preparing a competitive car. If you win everything at a rallycross weekend you can't hope for more than about £100 in prize money. If you do the impossible, enter all events in a season and win them all, your pockets aren't exactly bulging. Competing costs a lot, but winning costs more. As Peter Harper says: 'If it costs you £1,000 to put a rallycross car on the course, searching for that extra couple of seconds will cost you another £1,000'. The figures may not be accurate, but Peter makes the point well enough: competition is so intense and even that it takes a lot to capture those extra few yards of performance that make all the difference.

The rewards for a car manufacturer in terms of public impact must be infinitely greater from rallycross than from rallying. The name and model exposure is so much more concentrated. With, in the 1970–71 season for instance, a total of 4–5 hours television time devoted to rallycross, there's a lot of publicity going for the manufacturer who can get himself among the results.

The thrills and spills of rallycross come through well on television, and so they should: the sport was custom built for the mass medium. The organisation behind the coverage of a meeting is almost as complicated and extensive as arrangements for the meeting itself.

BBC coverage, for example, involves a total of about 45 people and planning begins well in advance of the transmission. Rehearsal is important because once the action begins everyone must know exactly what to do. The experts have got to work quickly and almost instinctively. There is only one chance to capture the thrills and excitement and if the camera misses a superb exhibition of driving, or a spectacular collision, the opportunity is lost for ever. You can't ask a chap to bash a car up again – even for TV!

The BBC use two cameras for rallycross, one a hand camera, and although the television team arrive at the circuit on the day before transmission, all their rehearsal is done the following day, as the cars are at practice.

The centre of the activity is the control van which is staffed by the producer, the producer's assistant, engineering manager, the sound supervisor and his assistant, the vision controller, and other important television experts. The control van, plus the radio links, which are also manned, are essential units in the complicated pattern which results in micro-waves being beamed to the Lime Grove Studios.

Practice is also important for the drivers at televised events. It's as fast and furious as the real thing, because practice times decide the drivers who will appear on television. Drivers and cars are well and truly warmed up by the time we sit down with an afternoon cuppa to watch rallycross.

Since the inception of rallycross, British Leyland vehicles, especially the Mini of course, have always figured prominently and they had their most successful season 1969–70. Out of nineteen events British Leyland cars were first home in sixteen. Works entered Mini-Cooper Ss secured five victories out of the nine entered, but it was left to the Sudbury fruit farmer, Hugh Wheldon, in his privately entered Cooper S, to gain the BBC/Wills Rallycross Championship.

This was the big event of the season the ITV series falling victim to the change of television programme contractors in February, 1970. British Leyland dominated the Saturday TV meetings with their works cars which won four times out of a possible six. 'Jumping' Jeff Williamson, in his first season as a works rallycross driver, won on two occasions with John

45

Rhodes and John Handley taking one each. In the non-televised Sunday rounds British Leyland works cars did not compete (proving the commercial attraction of the box for manufacturers!), but privateer Wheldon did and he did well enough at the Saturday events, against the might of the BL works boys, and also at the Sunday meetings, to take the championship. His positions in the eight rounds were: non-start; 7th; 4th; 5th; 2nd; 2nd; non-start; 2nd.

Minis also came out on top in the two Sunday Championship events.

Before the unheralded demise of their rallycross series ITV ran three events, two at Cadwell Park sponsored by Player's No. 6 and supported by Sunday Clubmen's events, and one at Croft sponsored by Guards. Two wins by George Jackson, and one each by John Rhodes and Brian Chatfield gave Minis an excellent four out of five, Timo Makinen in his Rally Escort T/C baulking what otherwise had every appearance of being a British Leyland sweep.

At the start of the season British Leyland competitions manager, Peter Browning, decided to put most of the BL effort behind the very reliable Mini S and the outstanding results of the season show how right he was.

Of course, the cynics would remind us that the Minis, with their wide wheel base and general design features, have natural advantages when it comes to the rough and tumble of the 'crosses', but even so the way they have dominated the sport is remarkable.

There were few dramatic technical developments during 1969–70 except perhaps in tyres where Rhodes and Handley experimented with a new handcut tyre based on the successful 12-inch CR 84 Mini racer. In dry and lightly damp conditions this type offered advantages and contributed to both drivers' victories in November.

Also on the technical side *High Road* the British Leyland magazine reported: 'In terms of transmission development most of the private owners appear to use the Ford-Salisbury

MK II limited slip differential, with specially made output shafts to fit Hardy-Spicer driveshaft couplings, and specially machined crown wheels, whilst a select few claim to be using British Leyland's own version of this diff.'

About development in the engine compartment, the same magazine reported: 'Only John Rhodes was seen with an eight-port head and fuel injection, which one finds most surprising as there must be quite a few ex-racing heads around which could be fitted with Webers in the interest of financial economy and reliability – cost and reliability being the two bugbears of fuel injection when used in conjunction with rough going'.

Then, in September, 1970, came the body blow. After all their involvement and support of motor sport, British Leyland announced their withdrawal, not only from rallycross, but from all branches of motor sport.

But even by this time the buzz in the business was pretty loud that Ford were going into rallycross in a big way; and with a proposed series on both television channels for 1970–71 and further rallycross possible for television coverage during the summer of 1971, everything seemed to be working to encourage their participation.

Into rallycross the mighty Ford went with the provision of four special Escorts and two special works 3 litre Capris with four-wheel drive for Robert Clark and brother Stan. This was considerably more than the one car for Barry Lee which had been Ford's contribution to the previous rallycross season. The reason? Said a Ford spokesman: 'Rallycross is bigger this season and we've more time'. At the end of November, another Ford car was provided for star drivers Rod Chapman and John Taylor and with the competitions department on the look-out to sign up a girl driver, Ford were certainly making certain of plenty of television coverage, whether or not they could in terms of performance mount a serious challenge to the rallycross genius of Harper, Wheldon and Co. in their smaller cars.

So, through the mud, dust, sludge and rain, rallycross roared into 1971, with the astonishing Hugh Wheldon in the lead in both the Wills/BBC and Castrol/ITV Championships. The latter series of meetings introduced for the first time to British TV rallycross a number of works supported entries from the continent to add to the interest.

Since 1968 rallycross has made a major impact on the continent, particularly in Holland, Austria, Italy and Germany. It has also captured interest in Australia and South Africa – so a European and even World Rallycross Championship may not be too far away.

More details of that exciting winter 1970–71 series of television events on both BBC and ITV is given in a later chapter.

4

Behind the Wheel

It takes a lot to tame a 'cross' car going at full tilt. Fifty or sixty miles an hour may seem puny against the speeds set up by the Grand Prix machinery, but at those speeds, in those cars and over that rugged territory, it's a man-sized job just keeping the thing upright and going in the right direction.

Much of the time, in fact, it's *not* going in the right direction and often you have up to all four wheels off the ground: but these are incidentals to be handled on the way. The real job is to keep pushing the car hard so that you are fastest round.

Autocross and rallycross make special demands on a driver's skill and technique. New situations come up quickly and have to be overcome with a versatility of driving not exceeded by any other branch of motor sport, except debatably rallying. All the time you drive on the limits – limits which are dictated by the ruts in the ground, the bends, the need to keep within the flags, the chap in front or behind, the mud, dust, flying stones and uneven ground. There's a lot more to it than putting your foot down hard and keeping it there. Judgements have to be finely made. Tolerances are acutely balanced. The borderline between a masterly taken corner and losing it completely is paper-thin.

In some motor sports the aim is to avoid sliding and

you're in serious trouble if you get too much sideways on. In autocross the approach has to be different. For much of the time the deliberate aim is to get the thing sliding and, depending on the type of car being driven, to cover some of the ground broadside. In rallycross entire corners are spent sideways on. It is all to do with balance and feel, which come from knowing what to do and how to do it. With a front wheel drive car, for instance, a driver will go into a bend with a fair amount of oversteer and with his foot off the accelerator, in order to get the car sideways on and pointing in the right direction for when he comes out of it. As he moves through the corner he'll put more power on, straightening up as he comes out of it. There'll be plenty of sideways travel going round such a corner, but if it's done skilfully and with courage, those vital fractions of a second will be gained which make all the difference at the end of it all.

In reasonably dry conditions the rear-wheel drive cars are often made to travel sideways as they come out of a corner at speed and will spend much of their time on the straight in vaguely this position, much to the delight of the crowd.

Mind you, it sounds easy, but there is a great deal more to all this than appears. Conditions are important and fine judgements are required if you are not going to slide too far or for too long when the ground is wet, or avoid a turn-over or inversion, as it is called in the game, when conditions are dry and/or the ground has developed ruts. Inclines too, both into and out of bends, must be considered and your technique conditioned by how much speed, slide, slip and braking they will take.

Here, autocross makes particular demands. Courses are temporary so there is little opportunity for a driver to get to know the layout of the course really well as a regularly competing saloon car driver, for instance, will know Brands Hatch or Mallory Park; or even a top rallycross driver, who will know Lydden like the back of his hand. With time for only a few laps of practice, many autocross drivers, in the style of motor cycle road racers, *walk* round the course to see how the bends go, what course conditions are like and where the loose soil, stones, ridges and similar hazards are situated.

At any especially hazardous section he will note the proximity of the marker flags, because taking these in the event will incur a five second penalty, though in practice he may well deliberately ground a few in trying to measure his technique against the limitations of the course in the prevailing conditions. He will also consider the best line to take at bends, again in view of the conditions, and try to establish how different sections of the course are likely to change as the competition progresses and in view of the weather conditions. It's not good enough to assume that a particular bend will take a certain measure of slide, simply because it took that amount of slide when you went through it $1\frac{1}{2}$ hours before.

An autocross champ is the chap who *thinks* his drives through – not the tearaway who blasts off, driving like the clappers. He has to know where he can get most help from the ground, at what points he can safely get a wheel or two up in the air, where he can gain from a slide and still keep on course, and the likely spots for overtaking.

On the other hand if you are a tentative sort of chap then autocross driving is not for you – unless you alter your style when you take to the course. Autocross driving is uninhibited driving and you've got to go quick and know how to handle it all *at speed* if you ever intend to get among the results. Brakes are the least thing you should worry about!

You have to learn cornering technique and the often ungentle art of overtaking or baulking because autocross, though fair, is tough and you can't expect anyone else to look after you once you're on your way.

A good start is important and if you can make that first corner ahead of the chap who started alongside, you're in with a big psychological advantage. To see a car ahead of you all the time can be cruel to your confidence and how do you overhaul him even supposing he gives you the opportunity?

Tactics are important and often the driver who falls behind from the off will press hard in the tracks of the chap in front in an effort to push him just that bit too hard, taking him off balance at the bend and, with luck, running him off on to the loose or at least making him sufficiently uneasy to spoil his concentration. Getting away first depends, obviously, on precise timing as the flag drops, but also on driving technique during those vital early two or three seconds; on whether you are driving on the good or bad side of the course; and on the degree of response you can squeeze from your car. It is by no means impossible to get home first, when you are second best at that first corner. There is still a lot of track left – and a second time round the lot; but it certainly makes life easier if you move out of that first bend, on the first time round, in front.

The experts make it all look easy and great fun so that the skills and the courage are tucked out of sight. It's a salutary experience to drive a car round an autocross course at just 15–20 mph. You don't really have to go twice or three times that speed to know what it must be like in the real thing.

Geoff Courtney, motoring correspondent of the *Evening Post*, Luton, discovering the thrills of autocross for the first time, described it as noisy, fast, even painful – but fun. He reported: 'The engine is straining to its noisy limit. Head and roof make regular contact. The steering wheel is bucking and the whole car sliding. Dust is everywhere. Bends are approaching much too fast, but left much too slowly'.

Geoff made his autocross debut in a highly-tuned Mini raced by Paul de Luca of Holmer Green and Ron Boughen of Hemel Hempstead. The 1962 bodyshell of the Mini had been completely stripped and later equipped with an 850 cc. fully race-tuned engine Cooper S head, 1100 rods, flat-top pistons, race cam and a twin-choke Weber carburettor, close-ratio gears and a locked diff.

Geoff climbed into this old-outside, new-inside Mini and after adjusting his crash hat, negotiated a few tentative laps of a course in Buckinghamshire which had enough twists and bends to test a capable autocross driver. Geoff worked up the revs, growing in confidence. 'Due to the noise and your comparative proximity to the ground there is a tremendous impression of speed, and people, blades of grass and grazing sheep nearby, are almost a blur as you thunder round,' he reported.

And at the end of it all: 'As I crawled out of the car my head was buzzing and my back aching from the continual pounding and shaking to which they had been subjected'.

Geoff's fastest two laps had taken 1 minute 13.7 seconds – just 1.7 seconds slower than Ron Boughen and Paul de Luca, but as he said: 'That's the difference between winning and losing'. And Geoff Courtney is no slouch when it comes to driving a car!

Who are the drivers who find this kind of exciting challenge irresistible? They come from different backgrounds, have different attitudes. Their skills vary, but they all share the same rugged enthusiasm for motoring over the rough. Let's look a little more closely at just a few of them.

Gordon Howie: Gordon moved into autocross in 1967 when he did small club events in a new 1098 Midget, but he smashed up the car during one of the Player's No. 6 meetings. He replaced it with another MG Midget and during the 1970 season achieved 12 firsts, 2 seconds and 2 thirds out of 16 starts, an excellent record. Gordon, unmarried and 25, works as a site engineer for a building firm and was sponsored during 1970 by Second City Developments, a building company in Wolverhampton. Gordon lives in Stourbridge, Worcestershire, and has ambitions to move into circuit racing in either Formula Ford or a large saloon like a GT Mustang.

Barry Lee: at one time or another almost all forms of motor sport have held a captivating attraction for this Coventry garage owner. Although only 25 in 1970 he had already crowded a lot of motoring experience into an eventful career. At 18 he was a speedway rider, having already had a go at stock car racing and go-karting, but an accident in 1963 put him out of speedway and, a year later, into autocross. He built and prepared a yellow Anglia and in 1964, 1965 and 1966 he won his class in all events. Driving first the Anglia and later an Escort, Barry won his class outright in both the 1968 and 1969 Player's No. 6 Autocross Championship. By this time he had also become interested in rallycross and his form attracted the attention of Ford, who provided him with an Escort. His ambition is to become a top rally driver.

Mike Hill: interested from an early age in driving, and with an obvious pride in driving well, Mike Hill won his class in the 1970 Player's No. 6 Autocross Championship going out to Gordon Howie in the championship knock-out. He entered his first autocross after he secured a Mini shell for £10 and through a friend acquired a 1275 cc. engine. 'I'd always wanted to have a go at autocross,' he declared. He started in June 1968 and at that very first autocross he secured the FTD and Novice award. He entered more club meetings in 1968 and a year later competed in the Player's Championship, reaching the Final of the 1000 cc. class after acquiring another shell and engine. Mike combines autocross with rallycross and has experience of rallycross in Holland.

Mike Day: winner of the 1969 Player's Championship, Mike has been active in motor sport for about twelve years, on and off. He started doing rallies, sprints, hill climbs, and then stopped until tempted back into competition by autocross. He used to navigate to start with on those early rallies and using first an old A35 and later a TR2. His first autocross was a BARC event at Eastbourne in an old jeep which had been used down on the Day farm in Kent. 'It was at the time that anything went at an autocross,' remembered Mike. Later came an old Turner with a 1349 engine and what Mike describes as knobbly tyres. Mike's great achievement came in 1969 when at Woburn Abbey he won the Player's Autocross Championship in a TVR Tuscan. What attracts him to autocross? 'It's a way of letting off steam. An exciting way of driving a car which you can't do on the road now!'

Laurie Manifold: doing autocross along with sprints and hill climbs as early as 1955, Laurie Manifold later discarded his MG in favour of a Volkswagen Beetle and entered the BTRDA Championship for the first time in 1961. He was among the first ten. He has remained faithful to the VW ever since and in the truly amateur traditions of autocross persisted right up until 1967 in driving to the event in the VW in which he competed. Altogether he has 'been through' a dozen VWs, and has spent more than he cares to remember on autocrossing – money, as he puts it, that might otherwise have been spent on luxury holidays, new suits, an electric lawn mower, and so on. But he's not really complaining. In 1965 Laurie ended the BTRDA Championship in fifth position and recorded twenty class wins during the year. Since then he has continued very active every season gaining many awards.

Profound dedication to the cause is the quality inherent in autocross drivers and Laurie Manifold has an abundance of it. As assistant editor of *The People* newspaper, he works in Fleet Street until 3.30 Sunday morning and a few hours later, having had no sleep and often having travelled straight to the meeting from his office, he is happily mixing it with the rest of the boys and generally doing well.

Gary Streat: one half of the famous autocross brother partnership of Gary and Brian Streat of Redhill, the early spirit of autocross still holds a particular attraction for Gary Streat. Entering the Player's No. 6 Championship for the first time in 1969, Gary said of it: 'It's okay, but it's not quite the atmosphere you get at club meetings. You don't know quite so many of the competitors and it's all a little more serious, which makes you more and more determined to do well'. Gary and Brian, with an old road-going Cooper S three or four years ago, had their first drive in autocross and found it

55

such good fun that during the following winter they built themselves a 1000 cc. Cooper S and started competing with it half-way through the 1968 season. Since then they have together won between 80 and 90 trophies. Now also involved in rallycross events, Gary says he has no great ambitions. 'I just do it for the fun and the enjoyment,' he says.

Autocross driving has to be learnt the hard way. You can't really read it all up in a book and expect to be doing FTDs in the first few weeks. There is no substitute for a sliding, bouncing car, as you fight to retain control. You can't simulate the mud or the dust; or the chap behind who drives too near in a desperate effort to overtake. You can't create the excitement, the tension, the exhilaration in any other way. You just have to get to grips with autocross itself.

5

All the Cars

Sit back, close your eyes and imagine autocross and rallycross. Ten to one a Mini comes sharply into focus. Since the days when racing over the rough came to mean something to the general public, and even before that for the increasing number of those much more closely involved, the BMC Mini (now British Leyland of course), has been the most easily recognised and immediately identified symbol of the sport.

And the most successful!

So successful were Minis in early autocross that someone had the bright idea of putting them all together in a class of their own, to give some of the other cars a chance.

Organisation had arrived, but the Mini went marching on, changing somewhat over the years, if not in appearance, then certainly in thrust, power and urge. The bog-standard 850, just scraping through now at the most local of meetings, has long since been inadequate for the more major events. Instead we progressed to the Mini Cooper and then on to the S-types, the most popular being the 970 and 1275 cc.

Quick to recognise the publicity potential of rallycross British Leyland spent money on the tuning of high performance Minis, and also 1100s, and entered works drivers for the televised events. The Mini Cooper S engine became a standard and most successful power unit – in the Mini, the

1100 and the 1300. Bored 40 thou. oversize to give a capacity of 1310 cc. and fitted with BMC 8-port crossflow head, compression ratio 13.5 : 1, it was standard in British Leyland's 1969 2-door Morris 1300 rallycross special.

This car's detailed specifications, carefully worked out by British Leyland's Competition Department at Abingdon-on-Thames in Berkshire, were as follows :

Power Unit: as already mentioned, with Lucas petrol injection, power output approximately 115 bhp. Close ratio spur gearbox, final drive 4.26 : 1 with limited slip differential. Oil cooler and auxiliary radiator fitted behind lower front grille, BMC extractor exhaust manifold, with short, large bore, tail pipe. Reverse gear stop on gear lever.

Suspension and Brakes: rear independent, modified to Mini-type rubber cone springs with telescopic shock absorbers front and rear. Dual brake master cylinder fitted with Mk II Lockheed swinging caliper disc brakes and drums at the rear. Magnesium alloy 12 by $5\frac{1}{2}$ wheels fitted with weathermaster-type tyres. Adjustable rear brake limiting valve inside car.

Bodywork: rear and side windows perspex, laminated windscreen, aluminium door, boot and bonnet panels. Interior alloy roll-over bar fitted, all standard trim, carpets, etc., removed. Fibreglas bucket driver's seat in steel tubular frame. Fuel tank fitted in middle of boot floor – 2 gallon capacity supplying petrol injection system via SU Electric pump. Mud flaps front and rear.

General: high output electric water pump supplying triple twin-jet windscreen washer nozzles. Leather covered steering wheel.

Although British Leyland have largely dominated both autocross and rallycross, many other makes of car have given exciting performances and gained many victories over the years. In the early days of autocross Allards, Morgans, Heralds and Dellows provided many thrills with, later on, Ford Anglias and Morris Minors. Later came the Volkswagens with a strong and successful challenge: and Specials, which had been around at the beginning of autocross in the unmodified form of trials machines, began to be designed especially for the job; and attracted increasing attention and interest, always adding spectacle and a touch of showmanship to a major auto-cross meeting.

It seems a long time now since those high-flying days when Open and Closed, with Specials – qualified as such only by two seats and mudguards – were the only classes.

In autocross everything takes a helluva hammering. Suspensions come in for the most brutal treatment and would be 'dead' inside five minutes, without special attention; that is if the car stayed the right way up that long. Autocross cars have their suspensions lowered and widened, to avoid the car from flying too high and wide off the ground and even turning over; but the 'all conditions' demands imposed on the auto-cross car can make the very features which are so desirable on dry days a decided disadvantage in the mud. The muck sticks more easily and in bigger chunks when the ground clearance has been lessoned. The result is additional weight and drag.

In most cases the extent of modifications to suspensions is determined by trial and error and generally some sort of com-promise is settled for.

The same goes for shock absorbers. Again autocross demands the impossible. They must be soft enough to absorb the bumps, ridges, potholes which, on many courses and at normal autocross speeds, combine to form an almost con-tinuous and often rapid jumping, juddering and bouncing. Yet they must be sufficiently stiff to handle the bigger bumps.

Autocross drivers need speed, of course, but of a special kind. The aim is to generate plenty of bottom-end power to give good low speed traction in the wet: and in order to avoid too much gear changing, which can be both a nuisance

59

and a hazard when so much concentration is necessary to keep the car going and pointed in the right direction, a flattened power curve is desirable.

Autocross cars are often dull, battered and dented, but it is a sport where pride of appearance counts little. What matters most is what you have beneath the bonnet. Can you imagine submitting to the full autocross treatment a car which was new, gleaming and unblemished? What that dust and mud would do in just one afternoon.

For the same reason, there's a ruggedness about an autocross car's handling characteristics. In the tussle to keep the car upright and pointed, most times, in the right direction, the steering will come in for some rough treatment. It has to be good and safe, but preciseness and finger tip control are as foreign to the autocross driver as is flying mud and rough driving to the Grand Prix circuiteer. Steering wheels tend to be small so that you don't hang about getting from one lock to the other.

No point in driving unnecessary weight around so most autocross cars are gutted of not-wanted heaters, carpets, door trims and similar refinements not needed on the voyage. Perspex windows reduce weight, though laminated glass is desirable for the windscreen because of the obvious risk from flying stones. A roll cage is important in avoiding damage to the car and injury to the driver should the car bounce extra hard and settle top to bottom; and it can happen so simply and quickly to leave a watching crowd open-mouthed. And a seat belt, preferably a full harness, is desirable.

Autocross cars, to comply with the RAC's regulations, must be fitted with a fire and liquid-proof bulkhead between the fuel tank and the driver's section, which usually means the sealing off of the boot.

Tyres tend to be as wide as possible with pressures around 30–40 per square inch when the going is really dry and down to around 12–15 when the ground is wet and squashy. Special tyres are not permitted and the RAC include in their Blue

Book a comprehensive list of normal production tyres which are acceptable for autocross.

Car preparation varies and is dependent largely on the car and the class to be entered. Vehicles undergo a series of modifications, often over quite a period of time and which are introduced as a result of experience. Resulting from successes in 1969 Gordon Howie, for instance, decided to replace the 1000 cc. motor in his MG Midget with an 1138 ex-works BMC unit, and to lighten the car with a fibreglass front and boot lid. The wheels were 5½J rear and 3½J front, fitted with SP44 Town and Country-type Dunlop tyres. The MG had Armstrong shock absorbers front and rear, and heavy duty rear springs which were fitted new for the 1970 season. Instruments comprised an oil/water temperature gauge, rev counter and ignition light, and other essentials were a bucket driving seat with full harness, roll over bar and aluminium steering wheel.

The hard top for wet weather could be removed, together with the screen, in dry weather. Other specifications: anti-roll bar at the front, panhard rod/radius rods rear, competition half-shafts and a close ratio/straight cut gearbox, with competition clutch. The five-gallon petrol tank was replaced with a 1½ gallon tank and the vehicle had two mini fuel pumps as a precaution against the failure of one.

British Leyland Special Tuning produced a printed leaflet once with the title: 'We'll bring out the beast in your car' and it is to bring out the beast in his engine, and that essential bite, that an autocross driver will spend hour after hour, over weeks and months, labouring over his vehicle. Gary and Brian Streat started building themselves a 1000 cc. Cooper S in November 1967 and finished it in June the following year. Devotion to the cause of most autocross drivers where their vehicles are concerned is quite phenomenal, the mechanical challenge of producing a championship autocross car overcoming the vast number of hours spent in tedious, painstaking and skilful work in the workshop.

61

Said Gary Streat, casually dismissing his and brother Brian's seven month solid labour: 'It took us a fair bit of time because we started from scratch and we'd never built one before. We spent most evenings and week-ends on it. We had several things go wrong to start with and it was quite expensive. We had to sort out the main problems and then get down to the little things and it was largely trial and error. Apart from work on the engine and other mechanical bits, the inside of the car was stripped out as is usual in autocross, with the rear seat where the passengers normally sit taken completely away. An aluminuim floor was laid from the seat back to the boot lid and fibreglass doors were originally fitted, but having rolled a couple of times, these shattered and on one occasion one of them clouted Brian rather hard'.

Always there is work to be done. Said Gary: 'After winning the class in the Player's final we got to work rebuilding the engine prior to competing at Lydden to gain an 8th overall and 3rd on aggregate in one of the events in the Wills Rallycross Championship'.

Mike Hill's class-winning Mini incorporates a 970S engine bored to make it 999 cc., lightweight and completely balanced. It is a 1959 shell deliberately because they were made of lighter gauge then. They were heavier from '61. The car has a fibreglass bonnet and boot, but not fibreglass doors. It has competition suspension with body seams welded and strengthened, and it is stripped completely inside – just seat, rev counter, oil pressure and so on, and the screen is laminated, with perspex side windows.

In an interview with Sales Link press officer Richard Feast, autocross champion Mike Day had interesting comments on autocross cars. In three years driving his TR he had two engines, as a precaution really because the first was not worn out. The clutch gave him trouble and, in Mike's words, the 'drive shafts on the back used to snap like carrots'. He had some specially made up and experienced no further trouble.

In some respects it all sounds very unscientific, rough and

casual, but the chaps who work on autocross cars know what it's all about and, furthermore, they know what works for *autocross*. It doesn't have to look pretty or professional. Everything must pay its way. Modifications, adaptations and improvements of one sort or another are all judged against the uncompromising yardstick of whether it works and whether it is better than what was used before.

You have only to witness an autocross car in action for just a few moments to realise that suspension is vital and this is where the work begins. Says Mike Day: 'If you have a standard road car you must tighten the suspension or you'll turn over. If you get a fast engine and a bad suspension you're going to be lucky if you don't end up on your roof'.

A full season of autocross takes its toll and the perils are there at every meeting. Though autocross experience is very much personal and individual, the Mini which competed during 1969–70 in the colours of the magazine *Auto Race and Rally* was perhaps fairly typical of the experiences of many of the cars which are tuned to take in autocross.

The magazine, reviewing the experience, declared: 'The Mini stood up to the season's hammering extraordinarily well on the whole. True, odd bits and pieces have fallen off in what might be called the normal course of events, but nothing really serious cropped up'. After trying first a 1275 head which fouled the water pump housing, a 998 cc. Cooper engine was fitted, there being insufficient time available to modify the block in order to retain the original engine.

The first problem was experienced at Theydon Bois, where what was described as a massive hump running across the circuit and which naturally had to be taken at speed (for this is autocross remember!) resulted in the gear extension breaking off at the differential housing.

Repairs involved lifting out the power unit and stripping everything down, because the offside drive shaft had sheared inside the wheel and the power output shaft had snapped inside the differential. The diff-housing had to be welded and

63

altogether the cost of the repairs was extremely high. As *Auto Race and Rally* explained: 'Some vigorous shopping around unearthed reasonably-priced parts, but a free-diff had to be used instead of the locked-diff system used up to then. This called for a totally different driving technique. With the locked-diff, the car could be taken at high speed, driven through the bend in a continuous slide, but still able to apply full power out of the bend. With a free-diff, the car had to be set up well before the bend and driven through, flat out, with tons of wheel-spin on'.

The next trouble was at Maidstone after abrupt contact with another Mini and attention was necessary to the glassfibre front end. Examination also revealed a nasty crack in the floor and this had to be welded.

In the last event in the Player's No. 6 Championship at Alwalton, near Peterborough, the Mini produced some laudable times in practice, but an ominous knocking developed in the engine compartment during the real action making further use of the car out of the question. There was extensive damage to the big-end bearings and the crankshaft, and an end-to-end overhaul was obviously necessary.

It all goes to show just how hard an autocross car is hammered during normal use. The price has inevitably to be paid when you regularly climb aboard and throw away your inhibitions on an all-out thrash round an autocross course.

One of the constant attractions of autocross is the wide variety of cars competing, not only one class to another, but within each class. Some of the cars may look similar, but virtually each car is individual once you begin to look more closely. The shell may be old and tatty – and invariably is because it is pointless starting off with something new when it is going to be modified almost out of recognition anyway – but in and around the dim and dented exterior is painstakingly constructed a car as individual as you are likely to find anywhere.

To improve performance first one component, then another,

Something from outer space? Just John Bevan and Naveb at Chepstow
Autocross 1970 on his way, of course, to FTD

It's Gordon Howie in front . . . and is that Dave Dawson just behind?

A kangaroo getaway for Peter Harper in the *World of Sport* Rallycross Championship. Harper in the 998 cc. Imp

Peter Harper climbs aboard

is added. One bit is taken out and a better bit put in its place. Whole sections are replaced in a gradual build-up which might extend over a number of years and perhaps include the changing of the basic shell a number of times.

Laurie Manifold, for instance, had his first Volkswagen in 1955 and in 1966 won the BTRDA Championship in a 1963 VW which had been progressively modified, year by year, to become the fastest rear-engined saloon of its time. By 1964 he was using larger inlet valves, half-inch made-to-order wheel spacers, a heavy duty clutch from a VW transporter and suspension modifications which included lowered rear springs, a specially strengthened front anti-roll bar and a set of Variflo adjustable shock absorbers. Laurie claimed that the Fish carburettor, which was bolted on to the original manifolding and said to be as effective as any two-carb conversion, gave a 20 per cent power increase.

During 1964–65 there were more improvements. The engine capacity was increased to 1298 cc., new rev counter and oil-temperature gauge were added, a close-ratio gearbox from a crashed Formula Junior car was fitted and, in an effort to give better handling, Laurie bought second-hand 15-inch Porsche wheels and oversize Pirelli Cinturatos. New shock absorbers, wheel spacers and an anti-sway bar just about completed the improvements at that time.

For 1966 the engine capacity was again increased, this time to 1470 cc., a special Blydenstein camshaft replaced the standard cam, the carburettor was rebuilt and a competition exhaust system and shock absorbers fitted. In an attempt to gain even better handling, Laurie had a pair of special 13-inch wheels made up with 5½-inch rims and these he used on the front with 14-inch wheels from a transporter with 5½-inch rims at the rear.

Inventiveness, resourcefulness, ingenuity, the ability to cannibalise with instinctive skill other makes of cars – all are central to the basic spirit of autocross and if the result to the uninitiated and uncommitted suggests a jumpled conglomera-

C

tion of assorted paraphernalia, then the justification is to be found in the challenge of building up something almost from nothing, in seeing it develop, in working out improvements and overcoming problems and, come the following week-end, putting them to the test in straight competition with others.

Laurie Manifold's VW, along with other Beetles of course, competes in the *Rear Engined Cars* category, where there is still a good proportion of foreign cars in competition. Out of the eighteen listed entries in the 1970 National Autocross Final, there were four VWs, three Renaults and the VW-Porsche of the celebrated Griff Griffiths. Eight foreign cars out of 18 represents not nearly such a high proportion as a few years ago, however, the main reason being the influx of Imps. There were seven in the 1970 Championship Final in addition to the Imp's stablemate, the Singer Chamois of John Homewood.

Volkswagens have been a familiar sight in autocross since the sport began and over the years have notched up successes of which many manufacturers would be proud. But the VW company is not interested in backing motor sport, so special competition parts are not available. The ingenuity of the VW autocross driver is thus often sorely tested in his quest to inject more urge into what is basically a rather ponderous vehicle as standard. Many a Beetle which comes at you through the dust has hardly anything other than its shell to show of its world famous origins.

Griff Griffiths' successful VW Beetle is Porsche-Carrera powered and the Bob Piper VW, as *Motoring News* so neatly put it when reporting Bob's efforts in the 1970 Final, 'has 1980 cc. of Ford V4 nestling cosily up to the VW's transaxle'.

Ford have nothing to complain about. Anglias and Escorts almost completely fill the traditional classes, the front-engined, rear-wheel drive saloons up to, and over, 1300 cc. They collect almost all the honours and a vast amount of prestige and good-will.

There is no doubt that at any major autocross the Specials capture a lot of spectator attention. Tough and hairy, their squat low lines and openwork framework are suitably in tune with the vigour and spectacle of autocross itself.

Specials in some form have been part of autocross since the early days, but as in most sports the limelight sweeps, picking out first one class and then another for the attention of the moment. At one time specials were unbeatable. Then the Minis came into the picture, getting faster and faster, and they were beating the specials. Then from the Minis and the many derivatives with increased engine capacities, came the Escorts to take over the glamour. Now the specials are claiming their glory again, especially with the boost given to the class by the outstanding success of John Bevan in his fabulous Naveb.

Fashion alone is not responsible for dictating the way events turn. It depends a lot on what is available in materials, parts, and of course, on how deeply a chap is prepared to dip into his pocket.

Howard Parkin is perhaps the most famous specials driver. He has been on the autocross scene for a number of years and holds the record for FTD – around 60 to date. His famous Cannonballs, the Mark 1 to Mark 4, have become part of the autocross folklore, although Howard has also been extremely successful in other branches of motor sport – hill climbs, sprints, driving tests. His present autocross Cannonball weighs $14\frac{1}{2}$ cwt and is appropriately named.

The demands imposed on a car subjected to regular autocross are always unreasonable and it is asking a lot of a basic, traditional road car, whatever modifications are made to it, to withstand the rigours and hammerings of an autocross meeting. It is being pushed far beyond the limits for which it was originally intended. In theory then, specials – simply because they are specials and are thus purpose-built for the job – should always have the advantage. But that's in theory . . . and many other influences decide which car will be best on the day.

67

Specials are not necessarily expensive to build, if you dis-
count the time, effort and heartache involved, but the creation
of a good special is a job for a special kind of expert. You
start from nothing so there is the opportunity to shun com-
promise in the design of the vehicle. You can build into it
the strength, the durability, the power, the control, the braking
and the safety factors in a blend which is specifically right for
autocross.

It is knowing what that blend is that makes all the difference
once the car is in competition.

Even so the expertise of the chap behind the project is never
guaranteed and many well-known specials drivers would agree
that some specials have been allowed to race which were more
suited to the scrapyard and were certainly extremely hazardous
at best.

The best specials cover the ground quickly. Howard Parkin
tells the story of Geoff Snow, one of the best saloon car
drivers in autocross and who later obtained a special. Reports
Parkin: 'I remember him coming in after his first drive in
his special and he was as white as a sheet. I said to him:
"What's the matter Geoff?" He simply said "God, I'd no
idea these things went quite so fast".'

The cost of producing and maintaining through the season
a really competitive autocross car of any kind is by no means
inconsiderable. Obvious items apart – the price of special parts
and frequent replacements because of the considerable hammering the cars receive – there is always the expense of transport to and from meetings, fuel costs, and occasional hotel
and restaurant bills if you want to do plenty of meetings. The
rewards, in comparison and even for the successful, are meagre
and generally require considerable subsidy before the books
can be balanced. Many autocross drivers are garage proprietors
or are in business in a trade associated with the car industry
and to some extent their rewards are to be found in the additional recognition and prestige which their autocross activity
brings for them at a local level. Others are farmers, who

seem to possess an affinity with the down-to-earth nature of the sport. Yet others – and there are many of them – are almost hypnotically attracted to autocross and continue to take part in spite of the commonsense economic reasons against it.

The excitement and satisfaction they derive from sitting in a barren car and belting it hard over a rough field is more than worth the cost.

6

Anatomy of an Autocross Champion—John Bevan

Garage proprietor John Bevan went to the National Autocross Championships Final at Peterborough in September 1970 with a big reputation. In his self-designed, home-built Naveb Special (Naveb spells Bevan, backwards!), he had registered seventeen class wins in seventeen meetings during the season and had secured a remarkable record of 18 FTDs in twenty outings.

A year earlier, at the 1969 National Final, John achieved second FTD and was placed second in his class.

But from the start, the 1970 Championship Final looked good for Bevan and with a series of scorching tours round the 800-yard course, and in beautifully sunny conditions, he drove commandingly to win all his timed and eliminator runs, setting FTD in a blistering 1 minute 07.26 seconds.

He'd reached the top in autocross.

John had de-tuned the Naveb's t/c engine, aiming at increased reliability, but he soon proved to any doubters present that the low-to-the-ground special still had plenty of go. Events seemed to be going in John's favour when Griff Griffiths in the Porsche Carrera-powered VW Beetle experienced steering problems in practice: and then when Colin Hargreaves, perhaps a serious contender for honours, had diff trouble on his Flymo, and Howard Parkin's powerful V6 Cannonball-Whistarni blew a clutch on his second run after establishing the second best time of the day, it really seemed to be John's day. All could have been serious contenders to his championship hopes.

This is not to say that John would not have won anyway, because he really flew round that Peterborough course and on the day was outstanding against all opposition. Derek Hearn in his 258 cc. Tiger Twin is not known to hang about, but at Peterborough on that day in September, Derek and the Tiger couldn't get within 14 seconds of Bevan's remarkable 2 minutes 14.91 seconds aggregate.

John remained devastating. After topping his class he was given an involuntary walk-over when Gary Streat's big Mini suffered transmission failure, but then he almost contemptuously disposed of Gordon Howie to reach the final. With Bevan and the Naveb in such staggering form, and set to face the less powerful V4-engined VW of Bob Piper in the final, everyone anticipated the result. With everything going so well for him surely only mechanical trouble could rob Gloucestershire John of the title now, but the Naveb was well up to the test. As *Motoring News* reported: 'Just as before, Bevan shot away from the starting area in a blur of dust and by the first corner all the unfortunate Piper could see was a ball of dust disappearing to a well-judged 7.1 seconds win and equally just National Autocross Championship title'.

For John Bevan the 1970 autocross season was superlative. A couple of weeks before the National final he shattered all opposition at the Farnborough DMCs Barley Mo autocross, taking the best time of the day and winning the knock-out championship amid giant dust clouds. Then, just a month after his exciting success at Peterborough, he travelled to Hereford and took the Welsh Championship, also gaining FTD. John's remarkable record for the entire season was

71

22 FTDs out of a possible 24 and two national titles. In addition, his was the first Special to take the Player's Championship title and he the first driver in four years *not* to come from the south-east.

What does it take to become National Autocross Champion? In John Bevan's case, four years of competitive driving, a special kind of car which cost just £250, and hours of hard work selflessly devoted to the cause by himself and his three helpers. John, 25 in June, 1971, owner of a garage at Brookthorpe, Gloucester and a member of the Forest of Dean Motor Club since its formation four years ago, achieved his incredible success in only his second serious season of autocross with the Naveb. He previously had competed in production car trials and special stage rallies with a 1650 cc. Anglia, gaining a number of class wins.

Before taking to cars John did a lot of motor cycle trials riding. One bike he made up from pieces, he called Naveb, simply turning his name the wrong way round. 'It seemed appropriate really, so when we put a car together from pieces it seemed right to use the same name'. At first John attempted to combine motor cycles and cars, but found there just aren't enough hours in a day, so he gave up the two-wheelers for the cars.

Perhaps the Naveb doesn't look a winner, but then what special does; and anyway, results count more than appearances. He had built a special before and, according to the Champ, the Naveb was a natural follow-up, though totally different from his previous machine. 'The Naveb took us eight months to build, working most evenings and week-ends,' remembered John. 'There was no master plan. We just pieced it together as we went along, building it up from scratch'.

The Naveb is plain, straightforward, but also stable and fast. John sits close to the ground, around him and forming a very 'put-together' looking frame, a chassis made from square tubing with old alloy sheet folded over the main members.

The suspension rides the bumps and humps untroubled, though there is nothing extraordinary about its construction – standard Triumph Herald at the front and mainly the front end of a Morris Minor at the back, with bits of VW.

Wheels seem just a trifle too big and are thinly shod with rough ground Michelins at the front and Goodyear Ultra Grip Rally Specials at the rear; on the Naveb, all very effective, the weight of the engine over the rear wheels pushing the tread of the tyres firmly into the ground.

Let's see what makes it all go. It's a 1558 cc. Ford twin cam engine, positioned at the rear, which has an almost standard compression ratio with usual 40 DCOEs carbs. The gearbox is standard Volkswagen with normal 1500 ratios. It is a very functional machine as results have proved and John isn't worried about its looks: 'We made it as strong as possible and weren't much interested in fancy lines. They don't help much,' he said.

The Naveb has an exposed Ford Escort radiator with sloping alloy pipes enabling the hot water to rise to help the working of the water pump, which is standard. There is no fan.

A lot of the car – almost too much it seems – is standard equipment, but the way it has been put together in John's space frame and the one or two secrets which naturally enough constitute privileged information, make all the difference.

John drives the Naveb in conventional style without concession to 'box office' performance and on the bends uses the sideways technique only when it is to his advantage or when it becomes necessary. That means in the wet. 'Because there is no weight at the front you can't steer round corners when it's wet, but otherwise there are no problems. The rougher the ride the better she likes it'.

The magazine *Car and Car Conversions* gave what appeared to be a romantic description of the car's design concept. 'Bevan had sat himself on the workshop floor (because with a nice low centre of gravity, that's where you are anyway), stretched his legs out to decide where the pedals had to be, the

73

positions of the wheels (or rather where they looked right to the driver), plus the seat. The engine and gearbox followed somewhere behind'.

But John maintains: that, virtually, is what happened, which goes to show the value of basic thinking and an unsophisticated approach to these things, even these days.

For a man who won more in 1970 than any other autocross driver, and with a home-built car too, John Bevan remains a very modest sort of chap. He makes a particular point of explaining that the Naveb's success was a team job and when you say how well deserved was his National title success, he simply says: 'We were very surprised'. He enjoys the friendly atmosphere which characterises autocross meetings and prefers galloping over grass rather than tarmac. He responds to the challenge of varied courses in autocross: 'No two courses are the same,' he says, and although he enjoyed Peterborough he added: 'It was a bit small'.

The future? Again John is modest and non-committal to the outside world. 'We're self-supporting and work very much to a budget, so we can't afford to have too much ambition. We'll probably have the same car, but with a bit more power'.

But with a chap like John Bevan, one can't help but feel that almost anything might happen.

7

Anatomy of a Rallycross Champion—Peter Harper

Peter Harper gained international fame as a rally driver. As a regular member of the Rootes works team he entered them all and did well in most: the Monte of course, and RAC Rally, the Acropolis, the Tulip, the Alpine. He has driven in the Tour-de-France, at Silverstone in saloon car races, long distance road races like the ill-fated Mille Miglia and at Le Mans.

Harper has been described as one of the most skilful drivers in the world on snow and ice. He was doing well in rallying when rallycross came along. Characteristically intrepid, he had a go. Since then rallycross, he openly admits, is his first love. Always practical, Harper explains frankly: 'Rallycross is less expensive and it brings you more publicity. In a rally you drive like a lunatic, are away from home for days and weeks on end and it costs you a helluva lot of money; and hardly anybody knows your name in the end. For years I was at the top in rallying, driving first for Rootes and then for American Ford. But just a couple of seasons of rallycross did more to get my name across to the public than all those years of top-flight rallying'.

There's a little smugness about the tone of voice; a slight natural arrogance about the direct manner of speech

which to those who don't know Harper well, could be mis-
leading. He's *not* simply interested in getting his name across
or in gaining maximum reward for minimum effort. He's
much too professional for that and as a professional it is the
challenge and the demands of rallycross which really lure him
to this new-type motor sport. 'Everything happens so quickly
that you've got to be on top all the time. You've got to be
away like a rocket at the start and there's always someone
up your backside, even if you are lucky enough to get away
first. Driving has to be tough and rugged and you've certainly
got to be able to handle a car pretty well to make out in
rallycross. A slight bloomer puts you yards behind with little
time to make amends. Inside the car it's hell. Thank God for
seat belts. At least they keep you the right way up. Outside
it's all mud or dust and you've got to bat along all the time.
It's not dangerous, but there's plenty of courage and skill in
rallycross'.

Peter Harper is a professional to his fingertips. He asks no
quarter and allows none. What advantages come along, or he
can devise, he grabs gratefully. 'At the start I'm happy when
positioned at the end of the line. Then I don't watch the
starter's flag or the lights. I keep my eyes on the other cars
and I'm away along with the first car that moves. If he's
jumped the start and doesn't get clobbered for it I'm away
with the same advantage.'

It is this relentless, uncompromising attitude which spells
excitement whenever Harper lets in the clutch.

His professionalism shows, too, in the little Imp which
he drives to success in so many rallycross events. Not for
Peter, the battered, dented, shabby-looking bodywork of most
rallycross cars. His attractive blue and white Imp is kept
superbly, shining always as it comes to the line for the first
event. It is generally by far the most immaculate model around,
and gleams like a beacon against the often tatty-looking models
he lines up alongside.

It says a lot for Peter Harper's all-round driving skill that he took to the Imp so readily. After piloting Rapiers, Alpines, Hillman Minx and even American Ford Falcons and Mustangs, the transition could have been a lot tougher, though he had a spectacular debut. It was at Lydden in the very first season of rallycross. Recalls Harper: 'There were four of us, a Porsche, Ford, Mini and me in the Imp. We were going up the hill on shale, it was before the track had been extended as now, when suddenly my windscreen shattered'. Not a very comfortable feeling.

Peter Harper's first rallycross Imp was a works rally car, 998 cc., and carried little additional modification. The same car was later developed by putting the radiator at the rear and eliminating the fan. Then Harper obtained a Frazer Imp with a 998 cc. engine, limited slip diff and, of course, it was very much lightened. For 1970 the Harper camp built their own Imp using a 1146 cc. engine, new drive shaft and going to 13 inch wheels (against 12 inches) with 7 inch rims. After a superb start, with Peter amassing important early season points, his car began to give trouble, mainly because of the extra power going through it, and a clout from Stan Clark's Capri at Lydden in December wasn't exactly what Harper had hoped for; as so often happens, Peter went immediately into the lead with Don Gilham chasing hard, Dave Preece in a Mini and Stan Clark in the works-prepared, *Daily Telegraph Magazine*-entered Ford Capri not far behind. With Harper struggling with car problems, Don went into the lead. Then it happened. Dave Preece's Mini caught the back end of Harper's Imp, Peter's Imp spun round, but only to suffer another clout by an advancing Clark in the Capri.

That put Peter Harper out and gave fruit farmer Hugh Wheldon the chance of making the fastest time of the day, without the worry of a serious Harper challenge.

It was a pity because the event which was the third round in the Wills Rallycross Championship, had begun with Peter Harper and Hugh Wheldon each with 19 points out of a possible 20; but rallycross fortunes come and go and plenty of the season remained for Harper to show his paces.

Says Peter: 'I like the Imp. It has weight where I want it and the rear wheel drive fairly pushes it round most corners, though the front wheel drive Minis certainly have the advantage when the course is greasy'. But the way Peter Harper drives this rallycross Imp no one could argue that it's a good car for the job.

While some of his opposition may be sceptical, Peter Harper insists that the Imp is privately entered. 'I get certain consideration and preference from Chrysler when it comes to obtaining parts and spares, and I also get help of this nature from other manufacturers; but I'm not sponsored by any means'.

Harper runs successful garages in North Hertfordshire and has been in the motor trade all his life. He's driven all kinds of cars, but for road-work still has a sneaking regard for the E-type. He competed in his first rally in 1947 and over the next twenty years gained hundreds of major awards. He rode his first Monte Carlo Rally in 1950 and did well to finish in the top twenty. He competed in the last ill-fated Mille Miglia and at Silverstone was involved in one of the most spectacular crashes ever witnessed at that illustrious circuit.

In his excellent book *Destination Monte*, Harper describes the incident like this: 'Paddy Hopkirk was coming through on the inside, got carried away and caught me a resounding thump. I spun round and Christabel Carlisle, following in a Mini, caught me. As my car rolled it picked Christabel's up with it and when the dust had settled there was the Mini . . . perched on top of my car. My first thought after my car had stopped was to get out quickly in case anyone else hit me, and was I amazed to see Christabel's Mini hanging up there . . .'

Always a driver of exciting technique, Peter Harper's talents are now witnessed by a much wider public as he throws the demon Imp round Lydden, Cadwell and Croft. By no means is rallycross all brawn and poke. The skills may be obscured by the man-size tugs on the wheel, the tearaway attitude and the outright abandon of it all, but the skill is there all the same and of that skill Harper has plenty.

Anticipation has always been important to the driving Harper. He thinks driving and anticipation should be inseparable. 'To drive well,' he explains, 'you must constantly *think ahead* of the car and the faster you are travelling the greater, of course, must be your anticipation.'

The ex-rally ace soon found out what it was all about in rallycross. As *TV Times* reported: 'Peter Harper takes Casino Corner at Croft (a 90 degree bend with a change of surface from gravel to tarmac half-way round) at speed, with his wheels turned into the bend – far too much for comfort. Reason? When he hits the tarmac the sudden extra adhesion puts the car on exactly the right course'.

Perhaps to some viewers Peter Harper's technique is undervalued. He may not slither and slide quite as much as some – the Mini drivers for instance – and because of this his tours may not be as scorching and spectacular, but this is because he knows not only the advantages, but also the limitations of his rear-engined Imp. Once the back end is moving on a rear-engined car it is difficult to bring it into line again, so the skill is to take it almost there and then hold it. Timings are a much more reliable guide to performance and in this department Harper, particularly in the wet, takes some bettering.

His last race in the second round of the Wills 1970–71 competition produced the Fastest Time of the Day – three times round the 1-mile long Lydden circuit in just 2 minutes 59.2 seconds, an average of fractionally more than 60 mph. Over that demanding circuit in these conditions that really is travelling.

Of the three regular rallycross venues, Cadwell used to be Peter's favourite. 'It used to be the most interesting from a driving point of view with plenty of ups and downs and swoops, but the recent changes there have made it too much of a micky-mouse circuit for me'.

Knowledgeable in all sections of motor sport, experienced in many, Peter Harper now concentrates his skills into rally-cross. His business interests take up much of his time, but as the summer draws to a close he turns actively to the new rallycross season. Modifications to his car, worked out and begun during the summer, are completed in September and October and then, with the first meeting imminent, the circus begins.

He'll spend as much time during the week prior to the meeting with his mechanic, Charlie Palmer, supervising vehicle preparation and, come Friday, he'll be on the road heading for Lydden or Croft or Cadwell. The competition Imp, clean and bandbox fresh, will go separately by its own transporter driven by Charlie.

Practice starts early on Saturday morning and drivers are in there for real, because practice times decide who'll be featured on the box later in the day. 'Exposure' to the viewing millions is important in rallycross because you'll not make a name for yourself if the viewers don't see you!

Then comes the real racing – tough, demanding, relent-less, and brash, over the mud, grass, gravel, cinders perhaps and incorporating a jump or two.

The winners build up points towards the Rallycross Cham-pionship. If you've done well you're happy. If something's gone wrong you curse, think about the extra cash needed to make the car more competitive, and promise yourself it's all just not worthwhile.

But then somehow, as the cars line-up at the next meeting and the TV cameras are focused on the line-up, you find yourself among them.

This is the world of Peter Harper, the expanding world of rallycross.

8

King of the Specials

You can't think of autocross without thinking of Howard Parkin. Once you get chatting about autocross Specials his name pierces the conversation like a torch beam bites into the dark.

The Specials are for characters and Howard Parkin is perhaps the greatest and the most durable character of them all – the uncrowned King. He and his famous Cannonball bring stirring action whenever they move on to the autocross scene. The crowd tense to the drama as he races his home-bred creation up towards the ton. Parkin is on hand and anything can happen.

Both on the track and off Howard Parkin is what autocross is all about. *How can you ignore* the chap who was the first to add a roll bar to an autocross car? 'Everybody called me chicken at the time. But chicken or not, roll bars, quite rightly, became compulsory'.

How can you ignore a chap who took part in his first autocross and wasn't even a competitor? That was in 1958. 'I turned out to watch a local meeting held on some land owned by my father. I was asked if I'd like to have a dart around the course. I was in my Sunday suit, but I borrowed a crash hat and off I went.' He was ten seconds faster than the current FTD!

This success inspired Howard Parkin's interest in autocross and his first competitive event was later that same year when he drove a Renault Dauphine to third in class. Eight months later he drove the Dauphine for the Midlands in the television inter-regional competition and won his class.

How can you ignore a character who pulls this kind of incredible, though innocent, bluff: 'To the Cannonball I added a lever on to the prop shaft tunnel. It was a bit of fun really and I only put it there to fox people. It was a rather large lever out of a Smith super 10 excavator. It had a cable which passed underneath into the prop shaft and on the end of the cable was a spring which was anchored to the chassis. The lever, spring and cable did precisely nothing and people used to see me come up to the line twiddling this lever.

'They'd say: "What's that Parkin?" I'd say it was my torque reaction lever and they'd go away nodding their heads very knowledgeably.'

Parkin says it was more than two years later that someone came along and rumbled the joke. 'I reckon you're having us all on,' he told Parkin. Howard said it depended on how you spell torque. 'If you spell it *torque*, then you're right. But if you spell it *talk* . . .' Howard Parkin's torque (talk) reaction lever was good autocross fun for quite a long time.

Who would *want* to ignore Howard Parkin because for more than a decade he has been an exciting and colourful part of the autocross scene.

It all really started with a garden power lawn mower way back in 1942.

Howard built a special two-wheel trolly to go behind it. He simply hooked it to the back and sat on the mower, while careering round a home-made track which weaved in and out of the trees in an orchard. Even at ten years of age, the Parkin inventiveness was showing through. Recalls Howard: 'After turning it over several times because it suffered from lack of wheel grip, the roller being of dead plain metal, I found it gripped a lot better when I drilled holes in it and drove 38 mm cartridges into the holes. It was good fun then for a number of years'.

Later he changed the gearing so that the mower would do 35 mph. Then took it out on a quiet stretch of road near his home, and the sight of this young lad perched on a lawn mower with throttle wide open gave an oncoming motorist the surprise and fright of his life.

Howard Parkin was only eight when his father taught him to drive. 'We lived on a farm and I used to drive an Austin 10 across the fields with a trailer on the back fetching turnips and stuff.' His first real road drive was a few years later, travelling through the middle of Sheffield one Saturday afternoon. His father commented calmly: 'If you haven't hit anything or anybody I think you're capable of driving on the road'.

Howard Parkin, the driver, was on his way. His interest in cars and motor sport developed. A very old MGNA with doors flapping, wings flapping and everything held together with string, was his first car. Then came an MGTD, a gift from his father, and this was to be the first of a number of Parkin-owned cars to receive 'the treatment'. On to it he fitted a supercharger driven from the nose of the crankshaft. The engine, the first to be bored out to 1500 cc., had alloy rods and it was supercharged at 12 lb. per square inch. Says Parkin: 'Its acceleration was phenomenal. I went to Brighton with it and did rather well and at one hill climb I shattered the class record by a considerable margin'.

With this success under his belt Howard Parkin thought he had everything that was needed to be a first class competition driver. After spending the next five years in motor sport and winning nothing, he had to change his mind.

During this time he drove a variety of tatty, old and obsolete vehicles and out of this mixture of odd machinery emerged what was to be the first Parkin special. He substantially modified an Austin Healey 100 M, fitting an in-

83

dependent rear end to the car, and although it didn't win anything, Howard had set course which was to take him to his famous Cannonball.

His first competition licence was taken out in 1950 but it wasn't until 1958 that he achieved his first major success. Driving a Renault Dauphine which by this time he had got revving to well over 8000, still with a standard bottom end, he did particularly well in Hill Climbs.

Howard Parkin was by this time obsessed by most branches of motor sport, autocross included, and at a BARC meeting, and in a specials car which had by this time become known as Cannonball to the few who knew it at all (for this was before Parkin and Cannonball meant anything in autocross), he secured second place. This was his first really competitive autocross event and he was very encouraged by it.

The car had been built with a strengthened chassis and into this had been persuaded an Austin Healey 100S engine which had come from the Donald Healey Utah-Daytona record car. Says Howard: 'The car was regarded as extremely heavy metal and very soon earned the name Cannonball. It started as simply as that. In a car weighing under 8 cwt the engine produced some 155 bhp, running on two 2-inch SU carburettors. It was the highest powered car I had ever handled at that time and would do zero to 100 mph in around nine seconds'.

With the heavy Austin Healey engine the car was difficult to manage and the engine was taken out and replaced with an engine which had won Trevor Taylor the Formula 3 championship. It was in this form that Cannonball gave second place to Howard at the BARC meeting.

Friday, September 29, 1961, is significant in the Howard Parkin/Cannonball diary of early events. In only the second autocross in which the two had competed, Howard took second FTD, only the then British Autocross Champion bettering his performance. As if to show it was by no means a fluke, Howard took Cannonball to the final autocross of that year, in October, and repeated his success, again only the British Autocross Champion ahead of him.

Until this time Cannonball had been a traditional two-wheel drive car, but in current autocross Howard Parkin is of course famous for his four-wheel drive Cannonballs. So how did the conversion come about?

Parkin smiles: 'As a joke really. Nothing more. After the October event we brought the car back to the yard to strip it down. Having got it stripped down I simply turned to my mechanic, Norman Lane, and said that I reckoned we could make the car four-wheel drive for next year. I said: "It only needs a diff sticking in there, a drive shaft coming out here and here, a mini upright there and there, a couple of springs dropping in here and here, and a drive shaft running down to the tail shaft at the gearbox, and I reckon we can do it. Anyway Norman, I'm off for a cup of coffee. Get started." I laughed and walked away'.

Two hours' later the laugh was on Howard. Norman had already made a good start and Cannonball, in four-wheel drive form, was on the way.

It was a joke which over the years brought much success and fame to Howard Parkin and Cannonball.

Cannonball first competed as a four-wheel drive car in April 1961. It wasn't perfect, but good enough to be only .3 of a second behind Frank Prior, the then autocross champion. Next time out Cannonball was supreme and then became virtually unbeatable. In 1962 when, as Howard explains 'we were really beginning to get the feel of things', Cannonball took 14 FTDs. There were 15 FTDs in 1963 and at least 10 the following year. At the end of 1970 Howard Parkin had 60 FTDs to his credit, probably more than any other autocross driver and it would be interesting to know just how far ahead he is of his nearest rival.

Behind this outstanding success hides a story of which the average autocross driver and spectator knows nothing. It's a story of trial and error, disappointments and frustrations, heartache, problems and near tragedy. But there was fun and laughs too. Parkin talks about it like this:

'When we started to test Cannonball in its first four-wheel drive form we were running on 15 inch wheels. We took the car up to the field behind my home. It was cold, frosty, with half an inch of snow – ideal conditions to go spinning all over the place. We set out a bit of a course and I thought we'd have a go to see how it handled, not having driven the car before in four-wheel drive form. I set off, went belting hard up to the first corner, put the steering wheel over, and went straight on, dead straight, and straight through a hawthorn hedge before I could get it stopped. I scrambled back, pride hurt and well scratched bodily, and we then sat down dejectedly to try to analyse the problems. It was true. The car would not answer in any direction at all. Whichever way you turned the wheel, however much, nothing happened. Further experimentation demonstrated that the car would go extremely fast in a straight line, but as autocross courses have kinks in them, we had to work hard on the car before we could finally get it to go round corners.'

Where autocross is concerned Howard Parkin has become the four-wheel drive specialist. Over the years with Cannonball he has tried some sixteen computations of all the variables possible with four-wheel drive . . . limited slip diffs front and rear; standard diffs front and rear; torsion bar drive to the front; torsion bar drive to the back; overrunning sprag clutches back and front; different drive ratios from one end to the other. He even bought a copy of the Ferguson patent from the Patent Office, studied it, built a layout to the Ferguson system and eventually scrapped it. A lot of labour, a good deal of expense, but Cannonball in the end justified the lot.

Then came near disaster. In a Chev-powered car he was using successfully for hill-climb events, he had the clutch explode on the change from first to second gear while travelling at the top side of 80 mph. The car shattered and Howard had a $\frac{5}{8}$ inch bolt driven half way through his foot. He was taken to hospital and operated on. Afterwards the doctor told him: 'You'll not walk again I'm afraid.' Parkin, well in character and typically forthright, retorted: 'I'll bloody well show you mate'. Within five weeks he was driving again and the foot gives no trouble. Says Howard, smiling: 'It just shows you that doctors are as fallible as autocross drivers, at least sometimes'.

Debris from the crash was spread over 200 yards and the pressing for the clutch pressure plate came out of the side of the car and embedded itself $1\frac{1}{2}$ inches in a telegraph pole. But no one, other than Howard, was injured and up to that time it had been only the second clutch explosion to take place in this country. The car was extremely fast and capable of reaching the ton from a standing start in under six seconds.

Autocross missed the character and colourful personality of Howard Parkin for most of 1968 – he was kept out of the game for business reasons – and he was able to do little, for the same reasons, in 1969; but in 1970 he planned a comeback in sensational fashion.

In the close season he had been working on a four-wheel drive, *four-wheel steering* special. Of course the idea wasn't *entirely* new. Back in 1926, in France, a four-wheel steering car had been worked on, but never saw the light of day. Later there was Freddy Dixon with the car he called the Crab, which had a definite mind of its own above 40 mph; and other people had tried out the idea without much success. Perhaps the most successful was that produced for driving tests and driven by Maurice Bishop which was, according to Parkin, a beautiful piece of machinery; but then, driving test speeds are relatively slow.

Howard's dream for 1970, however, never got to an autocross meeting. In spite of producing what was perhaps the only successful high speed four-wheel steering car ever, the bugs a-plenty which attended its development couldn't be sorted out successfully for autocross competition.

The intention was right. The bugbear of four-wheel drive autocross cars is that they understeer. The best way to counter this is to apply oversteer, and to make a car oversteer properly is to get the back end to steer as well as the front. That's the theory, but early practice – with autocross in mind – showed up the problems. Says Howard: 'The usual test of a stable car is to put it on a straight line, take your hands off the steering, plant your foot right down, and leave it to the car. If it's built right it should continue in a straight line. If not, all hell's let loose. We found, with the four-wheel steering car, that I could do a twenty foot circle with wheels spinning at something like 70 mph, leaving it entirely to the car. No matter what I did to the car, it kept going in permanent left hand and right hand circles. It took us a couple of months to sort out the problem, but by this time we had disconnected the four-wheel drive from the four-wheel steering and had started using it as a front-wheel drive autocross car'.

It was entered in about a half dozen autocrosses in 1970 and through corners became undoubtedly the fastest thing around, much to the consternation of competitors and the delight and excitement of the crowd. 'At one autocross I was going through a left hand corner at 108 mph, so the car was relatively stable.'

The swings and roundabouts principle applies in autocross as it does in almost all things, so while the latest Cannonball was phenomenal through corners, it lost ground coming out of the bends. The problem was basic to all front wheel drive cars – plenty of load transfer towards the rear, which is exactly what you *don't* want, because it takes weight off the driving wheels causing premature wheel spin. This means that although you go through corners at higher speed, a relatively good rear-wheel drive car will lead you out of the corners on pure traction.

Because of the lack of drive out of the corners, Parkin scrapped the car after about half a dozen meetings but, off the course, for some time, he and his mechanic had been working on a new version of his old love, the four-wheel drive car. A chassis was designed and made in model form by Terry Conner and much time was spent in designing the car virtually from the tyres upwards. 'We made no compromises,' reported Howard. 'The design and chassis is built to last, so much so that the car, which is powered by a three litre V6 Ford motor, weighs as much as $14\frac{1}{2}$ cwt, nearly twice that of a normal special.'

In its early stages it suffered from fore-and-aft pitching, but extra long radius arms were fitted and a third shock absorber – and the car was progressively developed during 1970 to the point where Howard says it was giving something like 220 brake horse power reliably.

'It is without doubt the best car I have ever produced.' At the early part of 1971 the car was undergoing its winter rebuild and Howard made this prophesy: 'When it comes out in 1971 it will be even faster, more stable, lighter and will be considerably more powerful'.

No one is more unashamedly immersed and consumed by his own specialised branch of autocross than Howard Parkin. Uncrowned perhaps, but undeniably, the King of the Specials, he talks with enthusiasm, from experience, and with a deep love of the game. His comments, on himself, on his cars, and on autocross generally are fascinating and significant as this random selection shows:

. . . on the treatment of Autocross Specials: Too many people build a special, race it, take it home covered in mud, stick it away and then bring it out and expect to race it the following week. Under the mud there may be a cracked frame or a cracked chassis; a cracked wishbone, a wheel pulling out or something like that. After every meeting my car comes in and is high pressure hosed down. It is checked over, every

weld in the chassis is inspected. Everything is checked –
wheels, hub nuts, bearings, engine oil, engine mounts, and
this *should* be done, not because something is certain to have
broken, but because something *may* have broken. Because at
the next meeting it may let you down.

. . . *on Cannonball 1 and Cannonball 4:* One year I worked
out that Cannonball 1, during testing and racing, covered
2,500 miles; that's 2½ thou of merciless hammer. At one
meeting I brought the car in with the chassis broken in
fourteen different places. But you learn as you go on. Cannonball 4, which will be racing again in 1971, has had no
chassis failures whatsoever.

. . . *on the design of autocross specials:* There is one funda-
mental point about the design of autocross cars which many
fail to realise. It is this: when you hit a bump with a wheel,
the wheel shouldn't hit the bump and take off to fly through
the air for a few feet, before coming down in a series of
bounces. It should ride up a bump and down the other side,
without leaving the ground. The majority of specials built
have inadequate wheel movement with the result that they
don't retain the wheels on the ground. If you fail to retain
the wheels on the ground not only do you lose traction, but
you lose the ability to control the car. My cars are built with a
tremendous amount of wheel travel.

The exact amount I prefer to keep to myself: but if you
see my cars go they appear to fly and the body remains fairly
stationary while the wheels are going up and down riding the
bumps at fairly high speed. There are times, of course, when
my car will become airborne – but that's not the object in
autocross.

. . . *again on Cannonball 1:* The first meeting we took it to a
little man came running up, stuck his head under the back,
and said, 'Oh, he's got drive to the back wheels.' He then
stuck his head under the front and said, 'Oh, he's got drive

to the front wheels.' Then he went running over to the scrutineer to try to get me banned before I'd even got the car off the trailer. Needless to say he was driving the slowest special at the meeting. As history proved, the car ran and everything was all right.

The first Cannonball was run up to 1967, by then having gradually put on a considerable amount of weight its power to weight ratio went down from about 180 bhp to the ton, to about 136. Likewise my girth had also increased slightly so we were fighting a losing battle. Nonetheless, at the Player's final in 1967, which was extremely wet, it was still fast enough on standard road tyres to make FTD in spite of Roger Clark and the works-Fords being present.

...*on himself:* I'm involved in agricultural machinery – I design and build agricultural machines – as well as building, and various other things. I've probably done more in four-wheel drive development than anyone else. Certainly I've had more wins in four-wheel drive cars and in them driven more racing miles in autocross than anyone else. I've planned and worked on a road car of my own and many of the lessons learned in autocross will be incorporated in the car.

...*on autocross:* It is essentially an amateur sport, though a few people take it very seriously. I take it very seriously because it happens to be my neck which is in the car. I try to produce a good engineering job and something which is fundamentally safe. Too many people go into building specials on a hope and a prayer. In my very early days, through my complete ignorance and inexperience, I suppose I did.

...*on why he went into specials:* I cannot think of one disadvantage of specials. You have a completely free hand to do whatever you like. Nobody can point a finger at you and accuse you of twisting or fiddling or having an engine bigger than you're supposed to have; or having something in a semi-production car that is not semi-production. These petty niggles to my mind take much from the sport of autocross and this is why I went into the specials class because I was given a completely free hand. I could build a special like anyone else and it was up to me to make it a success or failure.

...on the present Cannonball: Incidentally, my present car is the only oversteering four wheel drive car ever produced. The reason it oversteers is a pure accident. When we were building it we made a basic error. Something went wrong in a calculation which for some unknown reason worked out to the extent that it produced an oversteering car. What that is, is a secret. It has taken me ten years and more of hard work, plus a twist of fate in my favour, to produce what has happened. In itself it is so relatively simple – it is nothing more than a plain, stupid mistake, but it works.

...on his love of car competition: I've driven in driving tests, sprints, hill climbs, standard car trials, and circuit racing. I began circuit racing in a Lotus Elite and I've competed at Aintree and Oulton Park. I've even gone drag racing!

...on his early days in motor sport: The first meeting I attended was as a spectator when I remember seeing one of the early 'greats' driving a 328 BMW, spin on every corner, and still win. This was in the rain and it fired me with the idea that I must one day race. That would be about 1948. My great amateur idol in early days was Phil Chapman from Sheffield who built the fearsome Chapman-Mercury Specials.

I had a number of cars in the early days including the ex-Dobbs offset single seater Brooklands Riley. I also had an early Bugatti which I bought stripped in chassis form. The person I got it from had fitted a Bedford lorry engine into it. I did manage one drive in this vehicle but only one because the throttle jammed open and I went straight through a shed.

...on tyres: I believe that tyres should be fairly narrow to give them bite, fairly good cornering characteristics and to avoid aqua-planing on mud. Great improvements have been

made in tyres. Having produced an oversteering car where it is possible to hang the tail out quite considerably like Roger Clark with the Escort, it is necessary to have a tyre at the back that slides, yet one at the front that grips, without gripping too much. A tyre that grips too greatly in the lateral loading is the type of tyre that turns cars over. The tyres should allow the car to grip up to a certain point and then slide, so that the car doesn't turn over as it might otherwise do. With the original Cannonball, 12 lb. per square inch was right, extremely low: but with the present Mark 4 Cannonball we have gone as high as 40 lb. and more to keep the tyres stable. On the Goodyear we use something around 36 lb. per square inch which I feel is about right although I would prefer about 20 lb. per square inch, which would provide a certain amount of 'give' to the tyre; but unfortunately the tyre manufacturers are not producing anything that is sufficiently stable at such low pressures, even on the low profile stuff.

Howard Parkin and Cannonball intend to be around for many seasons to come: and that can only be to the good of autocross.

9

Man and Autocross

Autocross burrows beneath the skin and into the blood. It quickly becomes an obsession. How else can you account for the madness which men find in a sport which brings such small, tangible reward, yet for the driver with ambition, can cost so much.

Well known and much respected among autocross exponents is Richard Wharton, a farmer from Hepworth in Suffolk. Three years autocrossing unbalanced his books to the tune of £3,500 and although he won his class in the 1970 Player's No. 6 Championship and scored sundry other victories of which most drivers would be more than pleased, his return in straight cash over the same period was a mere £260. Any wonder Richard comments: 'You can see this sport is done purely for enjoyment. Perhaps on the merits of our success, some form of sponsorship will be forthcoming'.

Autocross makes prodigious demands on those who succumb to it: in time particularly, but also in finance and in specialist skill, courage and daring. It gives in return not the glamour success of the race circuit, but a deep, inner satisfaction, exhilaration and thrill, whether winning or losing. Richard Wharton and his mechanic Ron Evans of Norwich, are typical of the many driver/mechanic teams who form the backbone, the basis and the very existence of autocross. They give much

94

and ask little in return. Only when you talk to them does the deep, committed interest, the compulsive attraction to it all, the mechanical challenge in producing the best car for the job, and the sacrifices which are ungrudgingly made by man for autocross, come through.

They talk modestly about the endless hours spent building up their cars and knocking them out again in just a few hours of furious driving. With gross injustice to themselves they dismiss the skill and the courage required to race rough-shod over fields and against the clock. They'll elaborate without encouragement on what they assess to be a scrappy bit of organisation; become incensed with a bad starter or an unfair scrutineer. But get them to talk about the time the car rolled over and they were helped out, shaken, but unharmed, and the conversation dries up in a dozen words.

Autocross is for the fun of *doing*; and the spirit of the game comes through best when you hear the chaps who *do* it, talking about it; chaps like Richard Wharton and Ron Evans for instance.

Richard Wharton – on his career in autocross:

Ever since a young boy I have always been very interested in motor sport. Although I often went to race meetings, I never actually took part in the sport. I was a farmer and this seemed to take up 9/10ths of my time. It was not until 1963 that I joined a local motor club and actually began to take part in the sport. Competition consisted mainly of rally-ing and autocrossing in an Austin 1100.

In 1967, after being a spectator at various Player's No. 6 autocross meetings, I decided to obtain an RAC competition licence, complete an entry form and really have a competitive go at autocrossing. Although I did not gain any success at the Player's meetings I did win once or twice at local club meetings and by the end of the year my appetite for autocrossing was growing.

In the motor club I had a very good friend, Ron Evans,

and one day I happened to mention that I would very much like to buy an Anglia and prepare this solely for autocross. Immediately Ron was interested and suggested that he might help me in the preparation. This help was gratefully accepted and in the winter of 1967–68 we spent many an hour in the garage developing what we hoped would be a competitive car in the 1300 cc. class.

The season began with a win at one of the Player's No. 6 meetings and from then on it seemed that the car was faultless. Results were very encouraging all season and we found ourselves at the Player's No. 6 final at Silverstone, something we did not think, but secretly hoped, we would achieve. At the final, we came second in our class to Barry Lee in his very fast Escort, which at that time was a very new model on the autocrossing scene.

During the winter months many modifications were carried out to make the car even more competitive for 1969 when we set ourselves Player's No. 6 class win for our goal. However, after 14 wins out of 20 starts during the season, we had to be content once again with 2nd place.

After much discussion it was decided that the Anglia could be improved no more and to be in with a chance for 1970 we had to change to an Escort.

Out of 24 meetings during the season we claimed 14 class wins, 6 second places, were overall class winners at both the 361 Autocross and the Player's No. 6 Championships, and were second overall at the BTRDA Autocross Championship.

After three years in the up to 1300 cc. class the plan for 1971 was to enter in the over 1300 cc. class with the same Escort car but with an 1800 tc and/or B.D.A. engine.

Up to the present we have had no sponsorship whatever and all developing has been done by private means.

Ron Evans, the car's mechanic, on owner/driver Richard Wharton's Ford Escort 1298 cc.:
This particular car was built in early 1970. It started life

First round of the Wills Rallycross Championship 1970–71 and Roger Clark in the four-wheel-drive Capri sponsored by the *Daily Express* slides through a corner to take the lead from Eric Clegg in the Morris Cooper 1340 cc. Fastest time of the day was recorded by Hugh Wheldon

Stan Clark in the *Telegraph Magazine* sponsored Capri at Lydden

Whoever he is . . . he's flying high at Lydden

as LHD export model Escort 1300 GT destined for Ecuador but somehow missed the boat. When collected from Fords it was showing signs of having stood at the docks for some time.

The first operation was to completely strip the shell down to its skin. All the seams were oxyacetylene welded to stiffen and strengthen the structure. Glass fibre wheel arch extensions fitted, glass fibre bonnet, boot and doors added and then the shell was sprayed the final colours of red and black. A glass fireproof kit was added to the interior of the boot thus keeping driver and petrol separate.

A vertical rear shock absorber turret kit was added and suspension front and rear was then grafted on. This was twin cam suspension gear, being, we hoped, capable of accepting all we could get out of a 1300 engine. Lotus Cortina radius arms are fitted to the rear axle and Armstrong adjustable shockers also compliment the rear end, finishing off was a pair of 7 inch Minilite wheels.

At the front the main cross member is boxed and strengthened and modified to give negative camber to the front wheels. As previously mentioned, twin cam front struts are used with fittings available for adding two additional lever type shock absorbers if needed. The steering rack is heavy duty and of course had to be moved from LHD to RHD. The pedal assembly was strengthened and modified to accept another master cylinder as the original servo unit for the brakes were discarded. Internally the LHD dash was cut out completely and a new dash formed from alloy with vinyl covering and just the essential gauges and switches.

One or two pieces of trim were retained to maintain a civilised appearance inside, but of course the car boasts only one seat and a hefty John Aley alloy roll bar. This, incidentally, is modified to locate on the floor of the boot instead of on the rear parcel shelf. We'd removed that! All windows are perspex as are the headlight covers.

The wiring loom was scrapped and a completely new loom

D   97 made up with just the essential wires incorporated. The complete brake pipe assembly was also scrapped and a brand new pipe layout devised and made up passing inside the car to the back end and all clipped down inside the car with the battery cable and petrol pipe so leaving no wires or pipes under the shell at all. The battery had been placed in the boot to help weight distribution and make more room under the bonnet. The petrol tank had also been scrapped and a 2 gallon tank fitted in its place. An electric SU pump sits in the boot pushing the juice up to the engine.

Now the mechanical bits:

Gearbox is 2000E mated to an alloy Lotus Cortina bell housing and being driven through a standard GT 1600 coil spring clutch. The engine has been developed over three seasons of competition. Specifications as run at the Player's final were as follows:

Cylinder head. Reworked, polished and fitted with Silicon Chrome single valve springs, standard GT valves polished and reprofiled. Inlet valves fitted with bronze valve guides.

Rocker Gear. Hand made one-off job, shaft made from old halfshaft and pillars made from similar material, spacers between rockers instead of springs. Rockers polished and reshaped.

Cylinder Block. Fitted with Hepolite Forged Alloy high compression competition pistons. Bowl in piston design means that to increase compression ratio the block and piston tops have to be skimmed. Also recesses had to be machined in the pistons to give clearance for the valves. Con rods are polished, shot peened and balanced. Crank balanced as well complete with lightened flywheel and clutch. Cam shaft is a Piper full race shaft with offset dowel locating drive sprocket to obtain exact timing. Steel main bearing caps are fitted and with this set up we can safely use 8000 rpm – (we are a bit conservative about revs rather doubting this 'Did $10\frac{1}{2}$ thou with standard rods' stuff).

Carburation. Twin 40 DCOEs fitted to a Broadspeed inlet manifold. Ford competition exhaust manifold looks after the other side of the head. Carbs have 33 mm chokes with 125 main jets.

Ignition. Sports coil feeding much modified distributor cap due to machining cylinder block and therefore inlet manifold being lowered sufficiently to foul distributor. Cap was cut away and holes filled with Araldite and baked in the oven. Distributor unit is off Lotus Twin cam being without vacuum advance which is unnecessary for this application. Spark plugs are Champion N6Y.

Lubrication. Wet sump using twin cam sump well baffled holding 8 pints of oil. Ford high capacity and high pressure oil pump delivering 80 psi when cold and 60 when hot.

We've obtained a compression ratio of 12–1, a power output and maximum weight of which we don't know the figures but have found to be suited to this particular sport: although, of course, we could make do with a few extra bhp if you know of any going cheap!

*   *   *

When it comes to cars for autocross and their building and preparation, Ron Evans undoubtedly, and like the many other experts who toil painstakingly and often uncomfortably in draughty garages and workshops, knows what it's all about and in just three years he and Richard Wharton have established a successful partnership.

But as the car's owner and driver it was to Richard one had to turn to build up more of the character, outlook, personality and motivation of the average sort of chap who kicks up the muck, slithers in the mud and often gets lost in the dust, all on a Sunday afternoon. What more could he be encouraged to say about himself, his ambitions and his ideas in the world of man and autocross. This is how the questions and answers developed:

99

What attracted you to autocross?

Feeling that I couldn't afford to go circuit racing in the way that I would want, I was attracted to autocross by what I saw as the relative cheapness of the sport. This turned out to be something of a myth. Remember that £3,500 in three years? I have a feeling too that autocross attracted me because I am a farmer – and fields and countryside are close to me and part of my life. As a farmer I had to learn a lot about soil structure and how it differs in different weather; and you learn a lot about wheel grip when driving a tractor! It is all knowledge and experience that comes in handy in autocross.

What about your work and family background?

I have been farming with my family since leaving Wymond-ham Technical College. We are small farmers with 90 acres of land and about 500 pigs. We're hoping to buy a 250 acre farm, but I hope still to find time for autocross.

Have you any ambitions in autocross?

Yes I have. My ambitions are to win one of the national championships outright and to build the potentially fastest autocross car in the country. My ambitions at a lower level are simply to win the events I enter. If I thought I didn't stand a chance of winning I would pack it in straight away. Don't get me wrong though. I am not a bad loser, but anything lower than first place is considered a failure on our part. I think standards like this are very important if you are to do justice to yourself and to the sport.

Rallycross – any ambitions, views, comments?

I would love to have a serious try at rallycross, but feel that the only real rallycross car is the Mini, and I would need to have a backer with substantial funds before I would consider building a car of my own. Rallycross, I feel sure, is for the works and large garage entrants and not to be attempted by clubmen, unless they are prepared to lose a great deal of money.

100

What about autocross in the future and what makes you happy or disappointed at the way it is developing?
Although I feel sure that it is inevitable that autocross will develop into a more sophisticated sport with more money being invested in it by commercial concerns, I hope there will always be room for the true amateur who wants to use his road-car; but there must be a distinction between the club autocross and the national championships. I would like to see the RAC devise a system of grading for the national meetings whereby only the best cars and drivers are allowed to compete.

Another of my hopes is that organisers will not find it necessary to select the roughest possible course they can find. A car-breaker course certainly doesn't enhance the reputation of the sport with drivers; nor does it appeal to the spectators when several of the cars drop out through mechanical failures. A smooth course is usually a fast course and speed is more spectacular than bumps, which slow cars right down. I am also opposed to those people who keep trying to change the rules to make the sport more spectacular, i.e., by racing cars against each other instead of against the clock and racing four or more cars at a time. I cannot see autocross ever developing into a vast spectator sport like football, for instance. But this doesn't matter. Along with hill climbs, tests, etc., it forms a part of motor sport which now appeals to many people and it is my belief that many more will be attracted to it. Why try to change it too much?

How do you manage to fit autocross into your busy life?
I sometimes wonder about that myself. Farming is normally a seven day week job so I have to fit my autocross in when time allows. I always feed the pigs on Sunday morning, usually starting between 5 and 5.30 a.m. Being used to an early start to the day is an obvious help when you want time left for autocross. I like to wash and clean the car on Monday evening, and Tuesday, Wednesday, Thursday and Friday are spent on modifications and alterations, fitting the work in as

and when I can. Remember, we've got to keep the farm going! Saturday evening in the season is always a last minute rush to get everything ready for the Sunday meeting. Unlike most people, I get little chance to put my feet up and watch television on Saturday evenings during the season.

Any amusing incidents or noteworthy situations?
As a matter of fact, we did have a particularly interesting week in 1969. On Sunday we dropped a valve at Peterborough and when we took the head off we found we had three pistons at TDC: after removing what was left of the offending piston and half a con-rod we decided we would have to invest in a new bottom half. After some frantic phone calls when we arrived home we finally located Peter Gammon at Bagshot, in Surrey, at midnight and were relieved when he said we could have a complete bottom half engine. The following evening I went down to Bagshot and picked it up while Ron (Evans) got things organised his end, ready for machining the block, pistons and engine balancing.

Meanwhile we had decided that it was about time we used a hot camshaft and one was ordered from David Newman of Farnborough during Monday. On Tuesday I took the engine to Ron and he said it would be ready to assemble on the Thursday evening. This I could hardly believe but kept my doubts to myself, thank goodness. Incidentally it was number one inlet valve which had broken, the head travelling round the inlet manifold and sticking under number four inlet valve. Thursday evening Ron rang me to say that he had finished the bottom half and was ready for assembly if the cam shaft had arrived. It hadn't arrived and it still hadn't arrived by Saturday morning. By Saturday lunchtime we had given up any hope of getting the engine ready for the meeting next day. So Ron, off on a spot of pleasure, went to Lakenheath Air Base for their Open Day. Meanwhile I had found out the times of all the trains carrying mail into our local sorting office and also knew all the sorters personally. At 3 p.m. I phoned again and they said there was a round parcel for me and I could pick it up if I went to the sorting office. The GPO were most helpful and we were very appreciative. I told one of my neighbour enthusiasts to find Ron somehow and disappeared after the camshaft. I didn't know how he was going to find Ron, but I had problems of my own at the time. I learned afterwards that he phoned Lakenheath and actually spoke to the Base Commander and had an urgent message put over the loudspeaker system telling Ron to go home immediately. We worked well into the early hours and next morning took the car to Dereham and won our class by over 7 seconds and were third over-all.

On another occasion I was asked to give an autocross driving demonstration by a local unaffiliated club and in my anxiety to do a splendid job put the Escort on its side but luckily I just managed to bring it down the right way up. It was in one of my own fields and the local folk thought I was showing off, with everything all under control. Actually it was a bit sticky and the car dug a front wheel in and just went straight up.

On my way to a meeting in 1970 everything seemed to be going well. The trailer was towing beautifully and the Escort looked comfortably secure. A few moments later I glanced in my rear-view mirror and thought the Escort looked at a strange angle. The Escort hadn't been as secure to the trailer as I had thought. The car had slipped back, the rear wheels had dropped off the trailer and in this odd fashion – the four wheels of my road car and the two rear wheels of the Escort spinning beautifully – we were moving along quite well at around 50 mph, much to the amusement of my friend and fellow competitor David Lyes, who was close behind.

How do you spend your time off-season?
That's an easy one. Simply building cars. The winter of 1967–68 was spent building the Anglia. In 1968–69 we built a new engine and did further modifications on the Anglia. In

103

1969–70 we built the Escort – and 1970–71 engrossed in building a BDA 1600.

Richard Wharton and Ron Evans are individuals. You find them in East Anglia. But in your part of the country, in all parts of the country, there are the local Richard Whartons and Ron Evans, and this chapter, Man and Autocross, could well be their story too.

10

Round and Round the Circuits

You can map out an autocross course almost anywhere and in the early days that is just what happened. Even today the venues may stay broadly the same but the course – or the field! – changes. The farmer wants his field back, the ground gets too boggy for further combat, so the show moves off to settle a couple of fields away.

It brands autocross as an unkempt romany among the un-initiated. For those in the know, the fun is all the greater for a change of scene.

Courses are established by flags, nothing more permanent, and as the occasion demands they can be pulled out and stuck in elsewhere, even on the same field, to make a different course. There is no difference between the surface on-course and the surface off-course, so that if you overcook things you don't drop over the edge, as you might be in danger of doing in a continental rally; or crash into a barrier or bury yourself into a brick wall as are the hazards in circuit or long distance road racing.

Courses are flat, there being no deliberate attempt to create ascents or descents as in rallycross, and seem to average something more than 900 yards per lap. Cars race round in a clock-wise direction. Straights are long enough to enable drivers to return an exciting display of speed, and there are sufficient bends to test their tail-hanging technique. Most bends are right handers because turning this way is somewhat more natural for right hand drive cars, though courses do include a left hander or two so that drivers don't have it all their own way. There is not a lot of room, side by side, so bumps and shunts are always on the cards and add to the spectacle.

Twice round or three times is normal, with the best times counting for the results. Speeds can vary enormously depending on the conditions but are generally sufficiently fast within the limitations of the conditions to provide plenty of excitement and incident.

The scrutineering at an autocross meeting may be scoffed at by the smoothie circuit driver (how do you scrutinise a car held together with string!), but is taken seriously enough by everyone concerned, with standards governed by the purposes for which the cars are to be used. Badly turned-out cars – even in autocross – run the risk of default, even before they get on course.

Infringes and stoppages, once the starting flag has dropped, are seldom, though an overturned car blocking the course brings out a marshal with a red danger flag. What happens more often is that a driver will 'wild' himself round, turning in a great performance, only to find that he was disqualified at the start because he moved off before he should, or that the timing gear at the end wasn't working properly and the whole thing has to be done again.

The non-establishment of permanent courses is seen as a grave disadvantage by those who would like to see autocross more sophisticated and commercially-orientated, but most drivers are opposed to too much of this kind of development anyway, much preferring to do autocross for the fun of it, and if they can just cover their expenses so much the better.

In spite of this, however, some courses have developed a kind of permanency and Players, when organising their No. 6 Championship Finals, made use of some of them. They used the well known Firbeck House Farm course, near Worksop, and Studley Green, the home of the Chilton Car Club, where basically the same course has been used for years. As the only semi-permanent site in the London area, it used to be *the* Mecca for autocross at one time, though perhaps it is not quite so competitive now as it used to be. Laps are about 1,000 yards and the course is very undulating.

Down near Taunton, the Walford Cross course has also been famous as the home of the first national-type autocross before the days of the official National Championship events and mention must be made of Odiham, in Hampshire, the home of the notorious Barley Mo event. Here, after the barley had been cut, drivers celebrated by autocrossing four abreast during a day which produced a terrifically spectacular event. Armco barriers were part of the safety precautions at this popular meeting which, rumoured early in 1971, would alas be held no more.

The Hagley and District Club hold their August Bank Holiday meeting at their semi-permanent venue near Stratford-on-Avon, and the superb Dudley and District Club course near Sutton Coldfield was deservedly chosen for the final of the BTRDA Championship in 1970. The Thames Estuary Automobile Club have their first-class course near Southend and many other clubs up and down the country devise excellent circuits, both semi-permanent and almost totally temporary, which test the skills and courage of the most expert autocross drivers.

Borrowing land on which to run an autocross is often far from easy and more than one farmer has been escorted down to the local for the traditional softening-up process before the organiser received a firm 'yes'. In a sport as amateur as autocross, course conditions are certain to vary enormously one area to another. One well-known driver once described an equally well-known course as being like a wall of death: but in autocross you do the best you can for a venue and it is in the sporting tradition of the drivers that they make the best of it. There are few tantrums in autocross.

A good choice for a venue was the East of England Show-ground near Peterborough, used for the 1970 Player's No. 6 Championship Final. Criticised in some quarters for its location, the course itself was nonetheless good and wide, had long straights, a number of good right handers and a left hander or two, and was slightly undulating. A driver with a keen appetite for autocross has no right to ask for more.

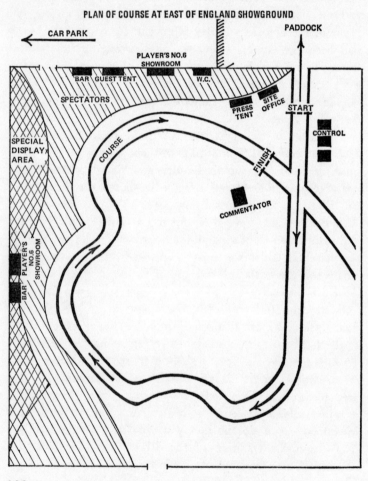

PLAN OF COURSE AT EAST OF ENGLAND SHOWGROUND

Rallycross, on the other hand, is much better off with permanent sites and circuits. It is easier for television coverage and much more manageable: the best camera locations can be worked out in advance and whatever structures which might be necessary in order to shoot the best pictures, can then be provided.

Viewers become accustomed to the layout of the course and this helps them to follow the action closely and encourages a closer liaison between the viewer and the sport, so essential to rallycross.

The three regular circuits for rallycross are Lydden, in Kent, where the very first televised rallycross meeting took place, Croft, in Co. Durham, and Cadwell Park in Lincolnshire.

Lydden

Famous Lydden was first opened for road racing in 1965, but for ten years prior to that it had been well-known for stock car and grass track racing. The first rallycross took place there in 1967. A rallycross had been held at Silverstone and when Independent Television approached Lydden to see if they were interested in hosting rallycross, the circuit management jumped at the chance and a good circuit was organised. Lydden has since become synonymous with rallycross in the public eye.

Lydden circuit came into being because circuit owner Bill Chesson felt that there was a real need for a genuine clubman's circuit in the south-east, to cater for as many different branches of motor cycle and motor sport as could be accommodated. In fact Lydden, in catering for motor racing, rallycross, car tests, motor cycle road racing, motor cycle scrambling, motor cycle speedway, kart racing and cycle racing, is probably the most versatile circuit in the country and almost certainly the only one personally designed and built by the owner. The design of the course places maximum emphasis on driving ability and machine handling, rather than on maximum speed produced by sheer horse power. For motor racing the fastest part of the circuit is Dover Slope where 100 mph is touched; on the rallycross circuit the fastest part is down Hairy Hill where drivers hit 80/90 mph just before braking for Paddock Bend.

Also on the rallycross course, Mabbs Bank consists of an earth mound so sited to ensure competitors keep to the rallycross circuit at Paddock bend. It is so called because Geoff Mabbs was the first driver to hit it! Chalk Bank is an extremely slippery section in wet and damp conditions. The Meadow brings many competitors to a halt in very muddy conditions while Devil's Elbow, as many viewers can testify, causes many exciting spins.

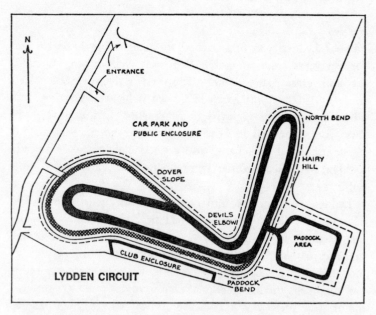

Croft

Promoted as the home of north-east motor racing, Croft Autodrome near Darlington constructed its rallycross circuit in 1968 to stage the *World of Sport* TV Rallycross Championship. This circuit uses part of the racing circuit, but a longer

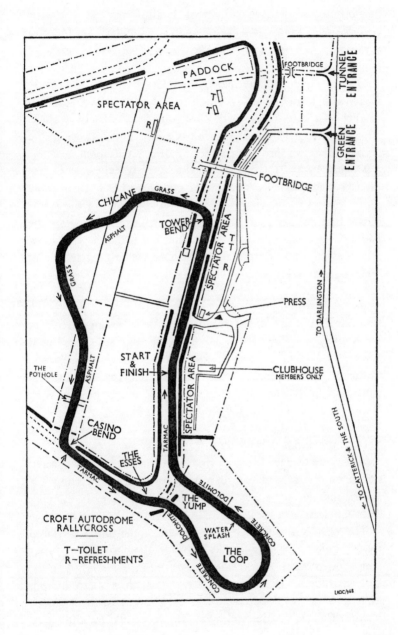

CROFT AUTODROME
RALLYCROSS

T – TOILET
R – REFRESHMENTS

proportion is specially constructed allowing five different surfaces, the 'Yump' which represents a hump-back bridge, and a water splash which is used providing there is no possibility of it freezing over.

Director and general manager at Croft, Mr L. R. Dixon Cade, says the circuit as a whole is a first-class test for both drivers and cars as the ever changing conditions of surface, and the sharp bends at Tower, Casino and following the Yump, allow no time for any easing of concentration.

During 1970–71 Croft staged the 'Guards Rallycross Championship' for which a number of changes to the circuit were made. Spectator viewing was improved by altering the start/finish line to beside the clubhouse enclosure, removing the paddock to a position adjacent to the inside public enclosure, and through the erection of additional viewing platforms at main vantage points.

Cadwell Park

Cadwell Park, the oldest motor cycle road racing circuit in the country, was founded in 1933. Twice lengthened, and used for car racing for the past twenty years, it became a rallycross centre in 1969 when ITV arranged two televised meetings on Saturdays in November under the organisation of the West Kent Car Club and the Cadwell Car and Kart Club, with the support of the Lincoln M.C. & C.C. Club meetings were held on the Sundays following.

A dry Saturday for the first event and a snow-covered circuit on the second Saturday made two very interesting TV shows and everyone was so satisfied that double the number of events were arranged for 1970–71.

The rallycross circuit consists of part of the tarmac surfaced road circuit, grass, and chalky cuttings all with many corners and gradients in a total length of approximately ¾ mile. The start/finish is on the road circuit with a sharp hairpin after 200 yards. Then comes a 1 in 9 ascent to the paddock inside 'Charlie's', descending with S bends to the steep descent in the cutting – the loose chalky surface – then a 1 in 8 climb on grass, with Yumps. This is followed by a right hand semi-circle to join the road circuit at the Gooseneck, a descent on the road to a sharp S bend and leaving the road, above Mansfield Corner, to a steep drop and sharp right-left on loose chalk and turf, with a Yump, to join the road again near the finish.

Easy? Then take a closer look at that TV screen the next time John Sprinzel reports from Cadwell Park. In your casual gear, with your feet up and a cup of tea in your hand, it's surprising how much courage even a Morris Oxford driver can develop!

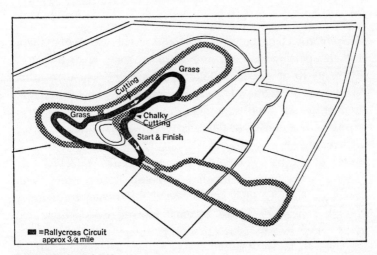

CADWELL PARK

11

Clubs, Competitions and Sponsorships

Many motor clubs now run autocross events as regular items in their sporting calendar and while in some areas autocross still tends to be considered perhaps less important than other club events in terms of the comparative numbers held, they are increasingly well subscribed and in many areas warrant considerable enthusiasm. Quite large crowds are often attracted to them.

One of the best known clubs with a regular autocross programme is the famous British Automobile Racing Club. With headquarters in London and operated throughout the country through a network of ten regional centres, BARC organised its first autocross in 1961. It wasn't a greatly auspicious occasion. Hardly more than 40 drivers took part and the crowd numbered little in excess of a couple of hundred. Now, with a total membership exceeding 10,000, about a dozen autocrosses are held annually.

In 1968 the BARC organised the first of their spectacular Autocross Festivals through their North Thames Centre. It took place at Hillingdon with a big and lavish programme.

Practice took place on Saturday, September 21, and was witnessed by about 450 enthusiasts, but the events the follow-

114

ing day attracted a crowd of well over 10,000. There was an entry of more than 120 drivers from all parts of the country, 240 officials and marshals were on duty, there were almost 30 trade displays, and altogether it was the largest and most ambitious autocross of the year, and probably the biggest event of its kind to take place in Britain up to that time. Profits were given to the *Save the Children Fund* and the event was sponsored by that excellent magazine *Car and Car Conversions*.

The event lived up to the expectation and there was plenty of exciting driving. For many enthusiasts Barry Lee in his speedy Escort 1600 provided the drive of the day, tearing round the course to register a time of 1 minute 36.8 seconds. This was an incredible feat, for Barry drove with hands damaged in an accident in his garage. Jeff Williamson in his Cooper S took his class with a fine performance in hard-fought timings with Pip Carrotte: and Jeff also took the BMC award for the best placed car in the event.

John Symons and Rod Hamilton had the crowd going with really close fought tours for the Duckhams Trophy, John taking it in his Symonspeed Riley Elf. Complete results in this first Autocross Festival organised by BARC were as follows:

Class 1   J. Williamson (1 minute 36.4 seconds)
Class 2   J. Symons (1 minute 37.0 seconds)
Class 3   T. Merridale (1 minute 39.6 seconds)
Class 4   L. Daubney (1 minute 39.2 seconds)
Class 5   J. Taylor (1 minute 38.8 seconds)
Class 6   C. Ramus (1 minute 37.4 seconds)
Class 7   A. Butcher (1 minute 40.6 seconds)
Class 8   P. Willis (1 minute 38.6 seconds)
Team Award: R. Douglas, P. Thorne, A. Wheldon (5 minutes 16.4 seconds)
Ladies' Award: Mrs V. Thorne (1 minute 46.8 seconds)
BMC Award: J. Williamson (1 minute 36.4 seconds)
Invited Drivers' Award: B. Lee (1 minute 36.4 seconds)

FTD (NT Member): R. Hamilton (1 minute 38.4 seconds)

FTD: P. Kerridge (1 minute 35.4 seconds)

There was no Autocross Festival in 1969 because it was only ever intended to hold the event every other year, but it was again organised in June 1970.

The weather was good and the conditions extremely dusty and while the event was keenly anticipated, it wasn't able to match the outstanding success of the first one. About 90 drivers took part and there were many exciting events, but the crowd was down to about 3,500. *Car and Car Conversions* again did the sponsoring and profits were in aid of the *Save the Children Fund*.

The British Automobile Racing Club is one of the oldest, largest and most active motor sporting clubs in the world. Starting life as the Junior Car Club in 1919, it amalgamated with the Brooklands Automobile Club in 1946 to become the BARC, since when it has been one of the pacesetters in motor sport. Its membership is spread throughout the world and includes many of the leading drivers. It now puts on an enormous programme of events covering every branch of motor sport and prints an excellent monthly newspaper for its members. The various Centres of the British Automobile Club organise a large proportion of the autocrosses held in Great Britain.

Another club supported by fine traditions is the British Trials and Rally Drivers' Association who organised a national autocross championship as long ago as 1961, and have staged it every year since.

Overall success goes to the most consistent class winner in a series of events. The Association was founded before the war and developed from an organisation specialising in Trials. Through the strenuous efforts of people like Bert Westwood, autocross interest developed and it wasn't long before the BTRDA were making awards to the best drivers taking part

116

in Autocross events. Before Players came on the scene, the BTRDA were running the most important national-type competition in the country and was really a distinguished and most creditable forerunner to the Player's-sponsored Championships. The BTRDA continued with their Clubman's championship and in 1970 an exciting contest produced Brian Moorcroft as the BTRDA Autocross Champion in a TBR Midget 1293 cc., but only after a run-off with Sid Davey which was so close that everyone wished they could have been declared joint champions.

The Taunton Motor Club also occupy a special place in autocross history because they were perhaps the first club to inaugurate a regular series of autocross events. That was in 1954, their regular August Bank Holiday meetings since having become quite famous. Other clubs in at the beginning were the Hagley and District Light Car Club, with that often-regarded very first autocross in 1947, the West Hants. and Dorset Car Club (1953), East Anglian Motor Club with their autoscramble in 1954 and, in the same year, the Cambridge Car Club.

Not to be forgotten, of course, are the combined efforts of the Sporting Owner Drivers' Club and the London Motor Club with their first autocross, held on Dunstable Downs, in 1951. It was soon after this that the SODC, according to Dr Pinkerton, who has been a member since 1949, ran a meeting for the Guild of Motoring Writers, who all travelled to Dunstable Downs to have a go. Reports Dr Pinkerton: 'Triumph's brought a pair of TR1s, which never went into production, for us all to try. Unfortunately, it poured with rain all day, and very few cars managed to get up the rather slippery slope on one part of the course, so for motor-sport the day was rather a wash-out, though the Gliding Club made an enormous profit on their bar takings! I remember John Bolster, who was our President, having a determined drive, and both Wilson McComb and Cyril Posthumus later became keen competitors, so the day wasn't wasted.

'Six or seven more meetings were held, enjoyed by competitors and spectators alike, but then the Lords Day Observance Society put an end to it all.'

Further reminiscences from Dr Pinkerton capture the flavour of the autocross of the day:

'At one meeting Frank Lockhart, who races the Rover Special so well in Historic Racing events, and I put on a demonstration "Match race" between his Bebe Peugeot and an air cooled V Twin Rover. One of his tyres on the Rover pulled off and went bowling away, so he drove hard after it, and managed to pick it up before it fell on its side! On another occasion when laying out the course in the late spring, my Morris Minor got slower and slower and eventually came firmly to rest, and nothing we could do would move it; we found that the long grass had wrapped round the prop-shaft and formed a cocoon which had jammed on the underside, and it took half an hour with a bill-hook to hack it free. We all had a lot of fun, and were sad when we had to pack up.'

Nor of course must the Farnborough and District Club be forgotten. They set off cars four at a time and four abreast at their Barley Mo autocross and have never been allowed to forget it. In the face of all the volume of publicity given to the Barley Mo event, it is curious to learn that the Thames Estuary Automobile Club (TEAC) claim to have run the first ever 4-at-a-time autocross at their $\frac{3}{4}$ mile course at Canewdon, just outside Southend. TEAC, a fine and flourishing club, was formed in 1949–50 as a general motor sport club specialising in rallies. As a rally club it became one of the most famous and at one time promoted the second largest club rally in the country.

With increasing restrictions on rallying, the club tended more and more to get off the road and on to the circuit and the rough. Their programme now comprises autocross, rally-cross (they are one of the few organisations in the country to run regular club rallycross), driving tests and race meetings.

A fine clubhouse and permanent headquarters are now established in Southend and the healthy membership of around 1,200 continues to grow regularly. About 150 TEAC members take part enthusiastically in autocross events.

Probably the most active autocross club in the country is the Chess Valley Motor Club based at Watford. Founded ten years ago, it now has a membership of more than 400, of which 75 per cent are competitive. Autocross figures very prominently in the club programme with members competing in events all over the country on a most regular basis. Breaking new ground, so far as an autocross club was concerned, was their excursion during 1970 to the Isle of Man when seven competitors in a total party of thirteen, participated in an autocross organised by Manx Autosport.

The club can add outstanding success to their enthusiasm and skill. Talk to them about it and they'll tell you proudly that in the 1970 *Watford Evening Echo London Counties Association of Motor Clubs Autocross Championship*, Chess Valley members took seven of the ten awards, in spite of almost fifty clubs being in competition.

Many other clubs up and down the country have done much to encourage and promote the sport of autocross and it is sad that space prevents warranted mention of them all. This chapter, in some small measure, is a recognition of all their efforts, but it would certainly be unjust to pass on without specific mention of the De Lacy Club of Pontefract who ran no fewer than *seven* separate autocrosses in a season, according to the 1970–71 Blue Book. This is perhaps a record for any club in the country.

The De Lacy Club, which derives its name from the history of Pontefract (Lord De Lacy was the Lord of Pontefract Castle), was already well established as a hotbed of autocross when the present competition secretary Robert Makin joined as an ordinary member some four years ago. The first autocross had taken place about 1960 and from the time when members used to take their old bangers to a nearby sand

119

quarry for a good thrash around, autocross, for the De Lacy Club, was on its way.

Now that same quarry, with a firm sand and limestone base, has become a permanent 920 yard course, slightly undulating and incorporating good right and left handers. An estimated £2,000 has been spent on improvements which incorporate permanent control buildings and toilets. The quarry offers excellent viewing facilities, providing a natural grandstand for the good crowd support which the club enjoys.

Said Robert Makin: 'We've invested in the course and it seems to have paid off. For two years we staged rounds in the Player's No. 6 Championship and are included in the calendar for the RAC National Championship for 1971. We also hold other sponsored events and we have the only course, I believe, in the north of England permitted to run 4-car-start autocross. Our present membership is between 180–200'.

A full list of RAC recognised clubs who ran at least one autocross event during 1970–71 is given at the end of this book.

*   *   *

Although much of the glory of sponsorship, quite rightly, has gone to Player's, with their financing of the National Autocross Finals for the period 1966–70, the sport has received a lot of support at a more local level by a host of companies, both large and small. B.P., Shell, Castrol, Guards, Jet Petroleum and even regional newspapers like the *Kent Messenger* and the *Reading Evening Post*, and Duckhams are just a few of the firms who invest money in autocross. Duckhams philosophy is typical of many of those companies.

Says their competitions department manager: 'Our policy towards support for autocross is similar to our policy regarding all forms of motor sport, which is to supply a small measure of help to as many up-and-coming drivers as possible, rather than to provide heavy financial backing to a selected few. For example, both John Bevan and Brian Moorcroft receive between 12 and 24 gallons of lubricants and we would have provided similar assistance to 30 or 40 competitors during the season'.

In addition Duckhams try to attend as many meetings as possible with their service vehicles to supply the lubrication requirements of any competitor using their products. The company also state that it is their policy only to provide support with the products they sell to the general public, and as they are continually taking samples of used oil from competitors, they gain information which enables them to improve their products.

Both Bevan (Player's No. 6 Champion) and Moorcroft (BTRDA Champion) used Duckhams Q20–50 multigrade oil, which is exactly the same as supplied to the general public.

Sponsorship, of event or driver, is now an essential part of the autocross scene and for those who sponsor there are good rewards to be obtained. It brings returns in a greater public awareness of a product and enables manufacturers operating at a regional or even local level to publicise their product or service at a fair cost. Facilities often include the sponsor's name in the title of the event and what is described as full on-site merchandising rights, banner and poster facilities, give-away samples to the crowd attending and, if you're lucky and can pay more, and want to go into rallycross, television coverage, which is still regarded very much as the exciting plum of sponsorship.

At one time motor companies and related firms, like tyre, oil, petrol and parts companies, were the only ones interested in sponsorship, but things are different nowadays. Cars and drivers are sponsored by individuals, organisations and concerns which have little, if any, connection with the sport. Gordon Howie for instance was sponsored during the whole of the 1970 autocross season by Second City Developments, a Wolverhampton building company. Says Gordon: 'This is real forward thinking on their part and will undoubtedly demonstrate to other companies in no way connected with

121

motor cars, the relatively cheap advertising this form of sponsorship provides'.

Sponsorship of this kind, while providing much needed and perhaps essential support, also adds a welcome touch of gaiety, colour and showmanship. Cars are emblazoned with names of sponsors and are brightly coloured in an attempt to gain public attention and recognition – all good fun and good business.

Is sponsorship good for the sport? Perhaps a more pertinent question would be: could autocross and rallycross exist without it?

Staging any event these days is expensive and certainly the cost of the major autocrosses would be prohibitive if sponsorships were denied. And at an individual level the value of sponsorship is highlighted by the well-known and successful driver Richard Wharton who, as already noted elsewhere, spent £3,500 in three years on his autocross machinery. During that time Richard, surprisingly because of his success, received no sponsorship; but how many drivers are willing to back their hobby to that extent without any financial help. That really is the measure of it.

Clubs are finding it increasingly difficult to stage any kind of financially successful autocross without some sort of sponsorship. Money comes in, but costs mount alarmingly too. But why? Where does the money go?

Take just one example, by no means specially selected to make the point, as almost any autocross club would testify. The Chess Valley Club at Watford organised a well attended autocross at their well-known Askett course on June 28, 1970. Total expenditure for this one event was £496. Receipts were £574. A healthy, handsome profit . . . on paper. But look at the balance sheet in a little more detail and you find that of the £574 income, no less than £155 came from various sponsorships, tied in with advertising, and awards. So without sponsored help, this highly successful event would have ended the day over £70 in the red.

122

The club has a sound reputation for organising ability, the weather was good, and an excellent crowd of almost 7,000 attended. Everything was favourable. But imagine the state of the balance sheet had it rained!

Some talk harshly about sponsorship, but in the commercial world of the 'seventies, is there really any choice if autocross is to survive and develop in an organised way?

12

Getting a Start and Moving Ahead

So you want to have a bash at autocross? Let's start with the car. Unless you want always to compete in the most local of events you must have a special car for autocross because it has all become so specialised now that your ordinary road car isn't likely to be nearly competitive enough.

But hang on – don't rush out with your cheque book yet! We've first to decide which class it is best to go for. Although you would face less competition in the rear-engined and sports car classifications, you would be able to pick up a Mini much easier and much more cheaply and this, really, is the car you want, for starters at any rate. One other thing: you ought to know a bit about what makes a car go, or team up immediately with a keen mechanic, because autocross is very much a 'do it yourself' sport and unless you have far more money than commonsense, the idea of putting mechanical work out professionally is unthinkable. And place orders for the specialist 'comics' too so that you can start immediately to read about autocross and begin to get the feel of it all. Many motor magazines give sparse coverage, but you'll find *Autosport, Car and Car Conversions, Motoring News,* and *Auto Race and Rally* good and probably best for what you want.

Formalities over, let's return to the car. You should be able to buy an old Mini for about £50 and you'll also need a trailer so that you can transport the car to and from meetings. You should be able to obtain a reasonable and perfectly adequate second-hand trailer for between £30 and £50 and while this may seem to be a rather fierce additional expense simply to transport your car back and forth, you must remember that in doing this you save money by not having to pay road tax on your competition vehicle.

Now the work begins. First the shell. You will need to strip out the car almost completely, inside. Dispense with all passenger seats, carpets, unnecessary trim (check with earlier chapters to see how the experts have worked on the insides of their cars), and make sure there is nothing that can roll about. Once you start putting your foot down on your first 'roughshoot' you'll find all hell let loose inside if everything you need isn't securely fastened down. More than that, it is foolish and dangerous to allow your attention to be distracted by such things. You must make sure your driving seat is really secure, for instance, and you need a full driving harness. Body seams need welding to help them withstand the rigours of the game without falling apart: and a roll-over cage is essential and will prevent you denting yourself! should you flip the car over. It will also help to prevent expensive damage to the body shell of the car. You'll need a good crash hat and make sure you *always* wear it, even if you have a private field of your own to practice in and there is no one present to remind you.

Suspensions are subjected to unmerciful treatment so they need strengthening with such things as a reinforcing tie-bar, pick-ups, and sub-frames; and you'll need competition shock absorbers. Wheels are important. Tyres too. Fit wide wheels. Town and Country-type tyres are important at the front, but not necessary at the rear.

You need a substantial exhaust system which will stay in one piece and you must have an additional tie-bar to keep the

125

engine from wandering when you're jogging up and down and side to side. Battery mountings need strengthening, for the same reason, and you'll need an oil cooler plus, perhaps, an additional water cooler. Remember that any autocross car receives cruel treatment and generally you have to make sure that everything necessary is done to stop everything falling off or apart.

You'll need a laminated windscreen and a fire extinguisher.

Many drivers have moved into autocross by using the car they are most used to, an old Anglia for instance or, more commonly now, an Escort. But the Mini really is the cheapest way of making a start so that you can enter the 865 cc. class. The S-type nowadays is essential to be really competitive in the big Mini class, but you don't need it in order to begin. First you've got to make sure that autocross is for you, so to begin with spend as little money as you need to have a fling, get the feel of it all and, most important, decide whether you enjoy it. Tune your engine to the best of your ability and, as mentioned earlier, if you are not too sure on the technical side of things, team up with a good mechanic who can work with you.

All the foregoing is not intended to be a fully documented brief on the preparations required for a car intended for autocross competition (for that you and your mechanic must read more technical manuals and talk to, and learn from, others competing in autocross), but it does give a general outline of the kind of specialist treatment needed for this specialist motor sport: but to complete the basic requirements to enable you to make a start in local autocross events you shouldn't have to spend more than about £150 to £175 starting from scratch, and that will include the purchase of your competition Mini and second-hand trailer.

Mind you, for this outlay your car won't be a class winning model, but with luck it can be modestly competitive and will give you a lot of fun. Most important, you'll be able to see if you have a real appetite for autocross and if you have, you can then go on to more advanced stuff, full race specification engines, and so on. You will have to spend money to win, particularly if you decide later on to contest the more major events.

While all this is going on you should find time to join a motor club and be getting the paper work organised so that when the time comes to begin, you are all set. Membership of a motor club should cost you about £1.50 a year, but do make certain in advance that the club you have in mind does, in fact, organise autocross. Though the sport is increasing in popularity, there are still clubs which do not include autocross in their programme of events, while many just have one or perhaps two a year. This might be enough for you to begin with. You are the judge of that, but if you want to be more active you can always join a couple of clubs.

If you want it is easy to compete in a great deal of autocross in a season, because closed events (which means that only members of the organising club can enter) are becoming less popular, while there is an increase in the number of restricted events (which means members from selected other motor clubs are invited to compete along with members of the organising club).

Ron Boughen, the autocross secretary of the London Counties Association of Motor Clubs and upon whose knowledge and experience most of this chapter is based, says that by being a member of the Chess Valley Club at Watford and also the BTRDA he can go autocrossing every weekend during the recognised season from April to October.

Before you can compete in autocross you must also obtain a competition licence from the RAC (the address is Royal Automobile Club, Motor Sport Division, 31 Belgrave Square, London, SW1) and at the same time invest in a copy of their *Motor Sport Year Book and Fixture List*, more commonly known as the 'Blue Book'. This comprises a wealth of information, much of which will be useful to you. There are the rules and regulations for the different events and lists of

127

motoring organisations and motor clubs recognised by the RAC. There is also a complete list in date order of all the events, including autocross, held by the motor clubs recognised by the RAC.

Now you're almost set, but don't jump in at the deep end and enter for one of the bigger competitions, even if you have the chance. Unless you have a field of your own to try in, you have to learn the art of autocross driving in the thick of battle, so obtain and fill in an entry form for a non-championship event and take things steady to start with. There may well be places for as many as 75 drivers at such an event, but you'll generally find, and perhaps to your surprise, that these just aren't sufficient for all those who want to take part. So pay your fee (around £1.50) and get your entry in early, because the general routine is, first come first served.

It's a big day, the first time you arrive to take part in an autocross meeting. You don't want to expose yourself as a novice – that might inevitably come soon enough when you get travelling! – so some knowledge of the routine is a help. Let's see what'll happen.

For a start, the notes you receive from the organising club will tell you at what time to report and on arrival you will be allotted a parking space in the paddock for your vehicle. Once settled you'll need to sign on at the secretary's tent, showing your competition licence and membership card. After that you'll have time to look at the car and do the odd adjustments before scrutineering, making sure that everything is in order.

You'll possibly have to drive into a special bay so that the scrutineers can satisfy themselves that your car is autocross-worthy. Quite rightly, and in the interests of everyone present, they will want to make sure that your car is safe for competition, so they'll be looking for wheels which might fall off, steering which is suspect, batteries which might not be securely held in place, leaks in fuel tanks, and so on. Once they are

Plenty of mud around . . . and plenty of strain at the front end

It's a girl's game too . . . as proves Rosemary Smith

Battling for a place at Lydden . . .

. . and at Croft

happy about these and similar points you'll be given a clearance and you're set then to do a few practice laps.

By RAC law each driver must complete at least three laps of practice before competing, but even before you climb inside your Mini, take a *walk* round the course. Look to see where the ruts are, how the ground falls this way or that, see where it's boggy, gritty, stony, and have a look at the weather conditions and try to assess what will happen as the contest develops. Try to make a mental picture of roughly how the course has been laid out, so that you have an idea where the bends come, how tight they are and how hard they might be to get round at speed, and the lengths of the straights.

Then inside the car ... and away you go. Don't go mad, because you look and feel a bit of a Charlie if you turn it over in practice. And there's no fun in breaking up the engine *before* the event starts. We'll come back to driving in just a minute, but first let's see how the routine develops. Practice generally takes place in the morning, and the event proper in the afternoon. You may be called for a drivers' briefing just before the official runs, but then you'll be in among the fray of your very first autocross.

Remember: if you knock one flag down you lose 2 to 5 seconds, depending on what has been decided for that particular event. For two wheels off the track you are down 10 seconds, and for all four wheels outside the flags you don't register a time at all. The average autocross nowadays will base performance on the outright fastest time and not on a time aggregate of the number of runs made. This means that if you are completely out of the running during one of your tours – you get all four wheels off, for instance, or your time is very slow – you can still win if you put up the best time in one of your other tours.

The average autocross afternoon will provide you with abundant opportunity for plenty of driving.

During the day you'll have three practice laps, two official timed runs, of three laps each, and if there is an eliminator,

E   129 you'll be hairing around again, and perhaps again depending on how well you do. There will be awards for FTD (Fastest Time of the Day); 1st, 2nd and 3rd Class Awards; there will be an award for the best time set up by a member of the promoting club; a team award perhaps; and there may very well be a ladies' award because more and more girls are becoming attracted to the sport. Altogether a full and exciting day – driving, chatting, watching and, above all, learning.

An increasing number of clubs now run a knock-out competition towards the end of the afternoon so you have chance again for more driving.

Even if you fancy yourself a good driver on the road you're likely to find 75 per cent of the entries at an autocross meeting surprisingly fast and when conditions are dry the speeds are pretty frightening for a chap new to the game. Don't be too discouraged. Unless you are exceptionally adept it will take you a whole season to learn the techniques of autocross driving and to get travelling really fast. It is simply a question of entering as many events as you can, becoming acclimatised to the conditions, the close noisy combat and the speeds.

These tips will help you through the awkward stage quickly:

1. Before blast off make sure doors are securely fastened, but don't lock them.
2. Sit securely and comfortably in your driving seat.
3. Make certain your harness is properly fastened.
4. A good start is half the battle. You must be able to assess the revs correctly so that you can move away like a rocket when the flag drops. Only practice will help you here. If you can find a friendly farmer try practice-starting in one of his fields. Practice those take-offs until you are almost jet-propelled.
5. That first bend won't be too near the start line because organisers like drivers to have built up quite a bit of speed by then, but even so you'll find it comes at you

pretty quickly and by the time you approach it you will probably be into second gear. You've got to learn to throw the car into the corner. It looks easy when you see the experienced driver doing his stuff, but at first there is the danger of flipping the car over. It's all a question of feel and reading the conditions of the track. Only by doing it gently to begin with, probing gradually the extent of what your car will take and what it won't, that you learn.

6. You'll hardly ever get into top, and hardly ever use your brakes, except in hairpins. It's best to know about these things before you start.

7. There is plenty of gamesmanship in autocross. If you happen to be first into that first bend you can of course use all the track which will enable you to take the straightest possible line through the corner, a definite advantage. You'll find too that some competitors will try to unnerve the other drivers by 'leaning' on them. This happens particularly in wet conditions, and when the course is tight and twisty. It's all part of the game.

8. If you happen to spin off, use your common sense and wait until the marshal signals you back on again.

9. Stop immediately on seeing the red flag. You will not be penalised and will always be given a re-run.

10. Take it easy in the paddock after your run. Anyone can put up FTD in the paddock, but it's not the best way to win friends and influence people.

Still keen to try? Of course you are so sort out that mechanic pal of yours, talk to a couple of local autocross experts, and keep your cheque book handy!

13

Rallycross Reaches Out

Rallycross had its biggest-ever show lined up for viewers during winter 1970–71. Both BBC and ITV presented major series with all the top drivers present and Ford making rallycross their scene in the biggest way yet, with their 4-wheel drive Capris and a team of four Escorts for a Ladies' Competition in the Wills/BBC/Lydden competition.

With Murray Walker (BBC) and John Sprinzel (ITV) on hand with their excellent commentaries, all was set for a great new season of rallycross and for those who wanted something extra there was plenty to enthuse about. On BBC the Capris faced a five second penalty on every outing, because of their natural advantage (particularly in certain conditions), while over on ITV we were promised exciting cars from the continent including some – like the Japanese Datsun – which would be making their debut on British television rallycross.

BBC moved us off to a great start on October 24 when, in glorious sunshine, we saw four identical Ford GT Escorts, with 1600 cc. engines, come up to the starting line: and here was something extra special for the viewers, for behind the wheel of each car sat one of the country's top girl drivers . . . Bronwyn Burrell, Valerie Norton, Carolyn Morris and Dublin's Rosemary Smith, who was fresh from taking the ladies' prize in the World Cup London-to-Mexico rally.

Straight into the lead went Bronwyn Burrell and although facing tough competition from both Valerie Norton and Carolyn Morris, it was Bronwyn still in the lead round the left hander at Devil's Elbow on the first of this three-lap race. Though visibly slower than the men – and quieter too because the Escorts were virtually standard models except for one or two comparatively minor modifications – the competition was good though it was still Bronwyn Burrell in the lead at the end of lap 1. But then Valerie Norton squeezed through on the inside and in a tussle for the lead with Bronwyn, out of the running went Valerie Norton as Rosemary Smith came through with a hot challenge. The Dublin girl, very experienced, was now sensing the chance of success. With just one lap to go, Carolyn Morris by now was right off the course and Bronwyn Burrell and Valerie Norton were falling back, so it was Rosemary all the way to take first place.

With the superb organisation for which television rallycross has become well known, the next four cars were already on the line by the time the camera swung round to record the start of the next race. And what a line up. Hugh Wheldon, driving his fabulous Mini Cooper and winner of the Wills trophy the previous year; Brian Chatfield in the Cooper; Tony Skelton in a Mini; and Roger Clark in the big sleek Capri. With a five second penalty and the four-wheel drive of the Capri surely not much advantage in the day's dry and dusty conditions, Clark would have to drive really hard to keep up with Wheldon and Co. Wheldon, predictably, shot into an early lead and as the five seconds ticked by Wheldon, Chatfield and Cooper got motoring while Clark waited on the line. Then he too, the five seconds up, roared away.

Clark in the Capri made tracks and was soon up in third place, ahead of Chatfield. Wheldon, meantime, was enhancing his rallycross reputation with some excellent driving and it was he, in the battered-looking Mini, who crossed the line first.

More races followed and in clouds of dust down at Lydden

a new rallycross season was well and truly launched. All the great rallycross names were to appear in that and subsequent transmissions – Jumping Jeff Williamson, Don Gilham, John Taylor, Pip Piper, Griff Griffiths, George Jackson and many, many others; and, of course, Peter Harper, the Stevenage garage owner with the great rallycross reputation. As Murray Walker told listeners at the start of the last transmission during that first of a new series of rallycross Saturday afternoons: 'If there is one man in this race who can challenge Hugh Wheldon, that man is in car number 44, Peter Harper'.

Harper, having had to pull out of the first race of the day with transmission failure, was out to make amends and as the cars surged ahead it was Harper, out in front, in the rear-engined Imp. As he tore round Devil's Elbow viewers could see the inside front wheel lift right off the ground, free wheeling, Murray Walker, with amusement, reminding listeners: 'That's one way to save time by reducing friction'. In front, with clear visibility, Harper moved further ahead and was still increasing his lead. Into the third and final lap and Peter was all of eight seconds in front. Could he beat the time of Hugh Wheldon earlier in the day, because the outright fastest time, and not the average time, had earlier been declared to be the deciding factor in this new series of Wills-sponsored meetings. Over the line at 2 minutes 47.1 seconds went Harper and it was close, but not quite good enough. So at the end of this first, exciting round in the 1970–71 Championship, Wheldon had nosed into the lead with a maximum of 10 points, with Peter Harper in second place just 1 point behind. Rod Chapman occupied third place with Roger Clark, Ron Douglas and Tony Skelton following.

But with five more events still to be run during the season, almost anything could happen and the big question was: what would happen in the wetter conditions when the four-wheel drive Capris would obviously have the edge over the smaller cars of Wheldon, Harper and others.

The second round, on October 31, produced even greater

speculation and more thrills. The conditions were wetter, which brought a revengeful glint to the eyes of the Ford boys; and scheduled to take his place in the line-up for the first time in the new season was John Rhodes from Wolverhampton, driving a fuel-injected Cooper S 1923 cc. engine, developing about 130 brake horse power. This car was reputed to have the ultimate in modifications especially designed for rallycross, and was probably one of the last cars to be prepared by the BMC Works at Abingdon for rallycross.

Could Rhodes and the Cooper S hold off the challenge of the powerful Capris? And what about Wheldon. Hugh would be determined to keep his top placing. And with only one point behind, the determined and skilful Peter Harper wouldn't be giving up without a fight.

The season was really hotting up!

As this second round opened it seemed the wet weather would give the Capris of Stan and Roger Clark, works prepared but entered by the *Daily Telegraph* and the *Daily Express*, an advantage, but the conditions soon dried out and the Capris were up against the odds yet again. Rhodes managed to gain 8 points but the fastest time of the day was established by the redoubtable Harper with Hugh Wheldon close behind. A tactical move late in the day came off for Peter. He switched to Dunlop racing tyres and got 6 seconds ahead of the best that Wheldon could do. The points table after this second round looked even more exciting: Wheldon and Harper level pegging at the top with 19 points each; Rod Chapman in his *Car and Car Conversions* Escort was in third place with 14 points, with Roger Clark in the four-wheel drive Capri in fourth position with 10 points.

Meantime, in the ladies' competition, with the fastest two drivers in each event qualifying for the semi-finals, we saw an exciting race with Viky Lincoln, a model from Highbury, who lost the car completely in practice, racing to the flag first with Tish Ozanne second.

Three weeks' later, with a switch of channel, we tuned into

the first of the 'World of Sport' rallycrosses on ITV from Cadwell Park, sponsored by Castrol with £800 in prize money. All the big guns were there at the start. Cadwell Park was wet and squashy after overnight rain as John Sprinzel came to the microphone to take us through the events.

It was raining and misty as the cars came to the line and then *off* . . . and down to the hairpin in the lead was Peter Harper in the Imp, with Roger Clark, Rod Chapman and Mike Hill chasing hard in that order. It had all the makings of another Harper victory, but the Imp seemed to be in trouble as Clark in the Escort came through on the outside as they came through the dip just in front of the start/finishing line. Harper retained second place for some time as a good battle developed for third between Chapman and Hill. Then Peter went missing and slipped to the tail-end as Roger Clark went on to win the event, though still outside the fastest time set up earlier by the redoubtable Hugh Wheldon.

The next race focused attention on the continental challenge with the 1500 cc. Daf from Holland, driven by the Dutch Rallycross champion, up against a couple of Minis and an Imp of sorts. John Homewood piloted the latter with John Boulden and Pip Carrotte in the Minis, but the little Daf, belt-driven with a Renault/Gordini engine, shot into the lead at the start, in what looked at this stage to be perhaps just another rallycross race. But wait, drama was just a few minutes away and central to that drama, the little Daf itself. It had just lost the lead when the spectacular collision with one of the Minis occurred and the little Daf went right over and back again on 'all fours'. With a battered roof the Dutch Champion turned the Daf round and, to the astonishment of most of the spectators, continued racing. With cars fighting for wheel grip in very deep mud and slippery conditions, all four cars were to have a bump of some sort before this race was over and in the end it was Pip Carrotte, at one time right at the back, who came home first, though his time was many car lengths short of the fastest time of the day.

An excellent slow-motion re-run showed what happened to the Daf on its spectacular debut in this country. As commentator Richard Davies explained: '. . . he's coming in and he's obviously overcooked it. He's not getting back in line at all and he hits that bank on the right hand side of the track and over he goes. The Mini comes in behind him, the Mini helps the Daf back on to his four wheels and the little Imp just creeps passed on the left hand side and of course they all had a crack eventually'.

A very eventful race . . . and still two more televised races to go. The next one was perhaps the most extraordinary of all. With conditions goo-ing up – John Sprinzel reckoned he'd never seen so much mud on the tarmac – all cars eventually shunted and as the event developed we had a most remarkable series of happenings.

Remember . . . ? It all started like this:

1. John Taylor, who was trailing in last position, ran into the bank with his Escort and had to be pushed out of the way;
2. George Jackson had a spin and shattered the back end.
3. Then John Rhodes, in the lead, blew up.
4. This left Stewart Brown the only driver left in the race and, although he didn't know it, in the lead!
5. Then Taylor got things going and he went into the lead, because by this time poor old Stewart Brown had gone missing. So John Taylor was not only leading, but now *he* was the only chap left in the race.

But more drama: within feet of the chequered flag, John Taylor stopped, reversed a bit, and then rumbled over the line to take the race, but not exactly in record breaking time!

This final drama left commentator John Sprinzel utterly astonished, but he delighted viewers with his superb entertaining commentary:

'. . . and here is the chequered flag, and why is he stopping before it – he's stopped before the line – the man's a maniac.

137

Well go on Fred ... cross it! Don't reverse you nit ...
oh well, never mind, that's the way to lose time. Any
minute he'll cross the line. The only competitor in the race.
He's probably stopped to tell Clerk of the Course just what's
going on ... but that was quite a spectacular achievement.
We can't tell how long he was because we haven't got a
calendar ...'

The next televised race brought in John Bloxham driving
another foreign car to add interest and excitement: the incredible Datsun, with over 200 horse power. Lining up with
John on the start line were Peter Warren, Andrew Cowan
in a 1600 cc. works Alpine and Bronwyn Burrell, in an
Escort, up against the boys in straight competition. Cowan in
the fibreglas Alpine, powered by a Renault 1600 engine, moved
into first place at the start and on the first lap had Bronwyn
Burrell close behind. Then John Bloxham took over second
place, seconds before riding up the bank, sliding and slipping,
but maintaining second place. Towards the end the racing got
excitingly close between Andrew Cowan and John Bloxham,
but Cowan finally went ahead.

In the final televised race of the day, there was yet another
foreign entry, a BMW brought from Germany specially for
the event, but unfortunately it wasn't the German's day. Rod
Chapman won this race in the Escort from Hugh Wheldon,
but ahead on the day by the time it was all over was the
great farmer himself, 'Hugh the Apple'.

Back on BBC, just a week later, and we were thrilled to
see further skilful and exciting rallycross, with the overture
to the event as electrifying as anyone could ask for in rallycross: Hugh Wheldon and Peter Harper would line up on the
grid with equal points, after two rounds. The compact Lydden
one-mile circuit would favour both these drivers with their
small cars tuned to perfection. Harper with his super Imp
1150 cc., tuned in his own garage at Stevenage; Wheldon, the
holder of the Wills' Championship with his 1300 cc. Austin

Cooper S, one of the fastest Minis in any conditions, and in his hands a potential winner on any circuit.

Furthermore, a change in weather conditions bringing the anticipation of parts of the circuit deep in mud by the week-end, stimulated interesting speculation about the big four-wheel drive 2998 cc. Capris of the Clark brothers, Roger and Stan, which are works prepared and entered by the *Daily Express* and *Daily Telegraph Magazine*. Roger, in the *Express* Capri, was at this point lying in fourth place with 10 points, and a win over the week-end would put him up with the leaders.

No viewer could possibly have been disappointed. The afternoon was filled with vintage rallycross – event, spectacle and drama; fast times, battered cars, exciting position changes, superb slides round bends and some excellent battles as drivers fought to keep their cars going at speed on the tight Lydden track.

There was Roger Clark getting the Capri all sideways on, losing it and starting again. There was Hugh Wheldon in his famous Mini which was now looking incredibly dull and battered (and not half the season over yet!). There was Peter Harper, with sensational impetus, rocketing into the lead and then Don Gilham, with some incredible chasing, actually snatching the first position while Harper tussled with a slide. We saw Brian Streat with his bonnet flapping. We saw Jeff Williamson with his door flapping. There was a snatch of wonderfully abandoned driving from John Geeves, and Jim Wicks belting hell out of the Anglia.

But the sensation of the afternoon was a three-car waltz which wrecked Harper's chances of piling on the points. As the little Imp spun it was clobbered by one of the Capris – and although Peter received nothing more serious than a shaking, it was the end of rallycross for him for that afternoon.

Although there had been some spectacular driving by the Clark brothers in these early rounds, especially from Stan, and no one could doubt that the big Capris had added interest and excitement to the rallycross scene, Ford nonetheless must at this point have been anxious about their first big bash at rallycross. With three rounds completed in this Wills Championship, the smaller cars had still found most of the answers to the demanding circuit in traditional rallycross conditions. Roger Clark, with 2998 cc. power in his four-wheel-drive Capri, was down in third place with 18 points. Hugh Wheldon, holding top position, was as much as 11 points ahead and even Peter Harper, invalided out of the third round because of the shunt, which meant he collected no points at all there, was still one point ahead.

Certainly, weather conditions had not favoured the Capri entries, but the change of fortune for which they had waited, was to come in the last televised rallycross before Christmas, in the second round of the Castrol Championship from Cadwell Park, televised in the *World of Sport* programme on December 19.

With the course drying out, conditions became almost perfect for the four-wheel drive Capris and they were to dominate the afternoon in sensational fashion. The Mini travellers weren't really in the picture and at the end of the day Jeff Williamson, in fourth position, held the best record.

Fastest car of all in this day of Capri command was driven by rally ace Roger Clark who, in some sensational driving, set up a new rallycross record, breaking the minute barrier for a lap over the tough, tortuous Cadwell course. He streaked through the radar trap on one part of the course at 80 mph and finished the day's racing in third position with a timing of 9 minutes 47 seconds. Ahead of him was brother Stan, in the *Daily Telegraph Magazine* Capri, with a timing of 9 minutes 43.2 seconds. Top honours went to Rod Chapman, in the *Car and Car Conversions* Capri, whose time was 9 minutes 30 seconds.

There was plenty of incident throughout the afternoon to keep the TV viewer wide awake. Chris Slater produced a very promising drive, we saw a privately entered Volvo with a bonnet waving to the camera, Jumping Jeff Williamson had us all going with a spasm of exceptionally quick driving in the ex-works Mini, and the Daf was on our screens again with the Dutch rallycross champion Jan de Rooy, driving the 55 Coupe into tenth position overall, the best performance from a continental driver.

Then in the last appearance of the afternoon for the Clark brothers, Roger was in the lead when he almost spun off the course and this bit of trouble let brother Stan through. Roger, regaining control, went off in pursuit of his brother, but one of the drive shafts to the front wheels broke and he had to finish his run with three-wheel drive.

For Rod Chapman, his triumph in this second round of the Castrol Championship, made amends for the disappointments he suffered at Lydden two months earlier. The *Car and Car Conversions* Capri in which he gained his success at Cadwell, wasn't ready for him to drive at Lydden so Ford let him have an old British Vita Capri, two wheel drive.

What trouble Rod had with that car. He didn't even progress as far as the actual event. At practice the accelerator jammed and a clutch pipe burst and marshals had to put out the fire caused by the fluid pouring out over the manifolds. Later in the day, Chapman raced his own Escort TC, won three heats and secured third FTD and second on aggregate.

But for the Cadwell pre-Christmas meeting, *Car and Car Conversions* had the Capri ready and Rod really made it go. It was a fuel-injected, 3 litre V6 engine making 220 brake horse power.

Meantime, out of television's gaze, the important Guards National Rallycross Championship at Croft produced a first round victory for John Taylor driving a left hand drive Escort, in the 'works supported' class. In the clubmen's category, Dave Preece made the best time, with Mike Hill, Mike Lawson and John Harris next in that order.

So came Christmas, then New Year, and rallycross drivers and fans looked forward to more speed, fun, shunts, surprises, adventure and spectacle at Lydden, Cadwell and Croft.

A complete list of final results in all these competitions is included at the end of the book.

14

The Crystal Ball

Life could hardly be better organised for the autocross/ rallycross fan. Through the late spring, summer and early autumn, autocross makes the scene. Then, rallycross, as the season sadly dwindles to an end, appears on our television screens to keep us excited, thrilled and enthralled, a shining light during the long dark winter months. So, for those who like their motoring over the rough – doing and watching – there's lots going on for almost all the year.

Even when the Ford Capris were fighting it out with Wheldon, Harper, Williamson and others, on both BBC and ITV, early 1971 saw autocross looking ahead to the start of a new season just a few months ahead.

Players, of course, had withdrawn their sponsorship and the RAC had decided to run the National event for 1971 without an outside sponsor. Early information suggested that twenty clubs would be chosen to run the qualifying rounds and that they would very probably include a smattering of new clubs. There were to be no eliminators, but whether scoring was to be based on aggregate or the fastest single run, had not at that time been decided. What was almost certain was that points would be scored in qualifying rounds to determine overall positions and that there would be no 'big time' National Final. Anyway, plenty for autocross to look forward to here.

Meantime the BTRDA were pushing ahead strongly with their ambitious plans for 1971. A new title and a new sponsor were sought and obtained with the result that we were able to look forward to the Castrol/BTRDA Clubman's Autocross Championship. Arrangements included twenty qualifying rounds and a final to be staged by the Dudley and District Car Club at a new venue. That was scheduled for Sunday, September 12. Some changes in regulations were anticipated. The two classes for sports cars would be amalgamated, bringing the under 1300 cc. and over 1300 cc. into one class, and the points scoring for the Ladies' Award would be eased to give them more chance of scoring points towards this award. A separate championship for club teams was also probable. The atmosphere and friendliness of the BTRDA Championships have always been something rather special so the organisers could look to plenty of entries and perhaps even greater stature for their competition in 1971. The 361 and Jet Petroleum championships were among other events to which autocross fans hoped to look forward during those dark-morning, dark-evening days of January, 1971.

Autocross regulations for 1971 were also changed to allow an increase in engine capacity from 3 litres to 4250 cc. Because of the limitation over the last two/three years in available power units up to 3 litres, this seemed to be moving the sport in the right direction, giving the lads the chance to get their hands on some good solid motors which would stand a full year of thrashing without their having to dig too deeply into their pockets or lifting the foot too much in an effort to keep the engine in one piece.

By now all these plans, in their final form, will have been run through with new champions emerging and new names making their mark for the first time on the autocross scene.

What of the die-hard rallycross boys in their works-entered and works-supported cars? Before the 1970–71 winter series a number of the star drivers went to the continent, where rallycross is becoming big, to test their skills against foreign competition. Jeff Williamson, Mike Hill, Stan Clark and others were there. John Taylor and Rod Chapman had been active in Denmark and Brian Chatfield had been to Austria and Germany. With the sport progressing very fast in countries like Holland, Austria, Italy and Germany, it seems feasible that this kind of 'home and away' season could develop even more for our pro and semi-pro drivers.

But what of the *real* future of both autocross and rallycross. What can we look forward to a few years from now? What would we like to see happen?

On the 'aggregate of two runs' controversy, autocross ace Laurie Manifold is not alone when he declares: 'I go for fastest run. I take the view that it is easier for the crowd to follow and you are finished if you happen to get a bad timing on one run'.

There is much support too for autocross following more the rallycross competition example with drivers building up points over a series of meetings.

More permanent circuits for autocross? There are problems, if indeed it is thought they are desirable, and planning permission would be necessary; but with more cash moving about within the sport, circuits of a more permanent nature might be set up as time goes on and in an effort to do more to capture a team or driver fan-following.

Speeds in autocross have gradually increased over the years. Says Howard Parkin: 'In 1964 at Colchester I was getting 78 mph down the straight – a very high top speed in autocross in those days. In 1970 at one meeting I was touching 112 mph and believe me, on grass, that really is motoring'.

It seems reasonably certain that general performance will continue to improve and, according to one autocross ace, the time has come when we can be considering autocross cars possessing a power to weight ratio of between four and five hundred brake horse power per ton. A longer term prediction from the same source: 'The time will come when we shall see exhaust turbo-driven supercharged cars running in autocross. This is a progressive form of power build-up and is far more controllable. The disadvantages of course are the cost and the weight of the extra supercharger, and the fine working tolerances which may not accept the amount of grit and dirt which is thrown around in autocross. But talking well into the future . . . it's by no means an impossibility'.

And rallycross? What is the future there? Certainly, with excellent viewing figures recorded during the early rounds of the 1970–71 series, there appears to be every incentive for television to increase its coverage, or at least to maintain it, and the numbers of ordinary folk who are now hooked on the sport, against a couple of years ago, is particularly encouraging. the big names of rallycross are now well-known to the general sporting public, and not, as before, to a minority of die-hard enthusiasts. They enjoy the thrill, the occasional spill, and with carefully thought out innovations aimed at improving still further the sport's 'box-office', rallycross could well emerge as a really big-time television sport in the next few years.

The arrival of Ford in a bigger way, with their Capris, has excited interest, and the sight of continental cars and their drivers in competition with our own heroes has been a boost too. The Ladies' Competition, though perhaps a little ponderous for the hell-bent enthusiast from the viewpoint of exhilarating action, has nonetheless added another dimension to the sport, and in anticipation of 'equal rights' and 'women's liberation' making an increasing impact on life in general, we may well see more of our girls driving rallycross cars, and not only in competition with one another.

Is there a place for Specials in rallycross? An old chestnut perhaps, but who could deny that the sight of Bevan's Naveb or Colin Hargreaves' remarkable Flymo hurtling round Croft or Lydden would create a minor sensation on the TV screen. They could well add a kind of 'show-stopping' special feature to the camera scene; and think of the excitement of close-up camera shots of 'exposed' drivers sitting on top of their creations, struggling to keep them under control at Devil's Elbow and Hairy Hill. Some of the Specials boys reckon they could thrash the backsides off most rallycross cars, and Parkin, in the true 'give-it-to-'em' spirit of the sport says: 'I could give Fords five seconds start and play with them'.

The problems associated with the admission of Specials into rallycross are obvious. How do you save the neck of a Special's driver in a shunt? He's in a dangerously exposed position and the torturous nature of rallycross circuits may well prove too much, too often, for the 'hairy ones'. How would the major car manufacturers take to the challenge from these 'creatures from another world'? That's another problem. But perhaps in time, Specials somehow, somewhere, might find a place in rallycross.

What is tedious about much of present-day rallycross on television is the series of snippets to which the viewer is subjected. We flash to the circuit for a couple of rapid races, then back to our continuity man in the studio before shooting off for racing at Catterick or Ascot, then swimming, indoor athletics or table tennis, before going back to Lydden for a couple more races. Hands up all who would like to see a more concentrated coverage, say 30 minutes of rallycross during the afternoon, *but 30 minutes all at once*. There are problems in this for the programme planners, because soccer (with goals being broadcast almost as they happen) and racing, take the lion's share of television sport time; and there are so many different events going on during any average Saturday afternoon that both BBC and ITV prefer to spread their sports coverage. But do bits of this here, bits of that there *really* satisfy anyone? All this is part of a more major problem of how to deal with sport generally on television.

Looking into the crystal ball is fascinating, but not always reliable: and anyway, the present is often much more exciting.

147

While it is right to look ahead so that autocross and rallycross can be developed along lines which are good for the sport, for those who participate and those who watch, the rugged and realistic nature of racing over the rough means much more concern with the fun and the excitement and the comradeship of *now*.

One of the most encouraging signs for the long-term future of the sport is the increasing numbers of younger people taking an active interest. They possess road cars of their own early nowadays; they like to know how things work; and many of them find a suitable outlet for their desire to be part of motor sport in autocross.

Perhaps the forerunner to many more events of a similar kind is the Junior Autocross organised by the Braintree Youth Motor Club. From Chelmsford a letter explains the idea like this: 'An unusual sporting event which takes place twice a year in Essex is Junior Autocross. As the name suggests this is "normal" Autocross, the difference being that children drive, and adults watch!

'It was started two years ago by Braintree garage owner Alec Lobb, who formed the Braintree Youth Motor Club, with the help and enthusiasm of his two sons and twenty budding "Clarks".

'They organised their first event in 1968, inviting Braintree schools to enter teams of six children. Amongst the seven teams to enter was the Boreham Boys' team, headed by Mike Meade, son of well-known AVO man, Bill Meade. Four more very successful meets have been held since then, a record crowd of 2,000 being recorded on one occasion.

'There are two main classes for the cars. The Specials can be any four-wheeled vehicle with a Ford side-valve engine up to and including the 100E, the Standard class including any Ford saloon up to and including the 100E, but excluding the V8 Pilot, with no modifications allowed whatsoever. These two classes are then subdivided into three age groups, 10–12,

12–16 and 10–16, girls only, the average age of prize winners at the last event being 14!' The letter is reproduced by permission of *Car and Car Conversions*.

The sport attracts and breeds a special kind of fellowship, fabulous characters, extraordinary enthusiasm, and extreme dedication. It is these basic qualities which the future of the sport, however it might develop, must preserve.

Appendix 1

RESULTS RALLYCROSS 1970-71 SERIES

BBC/Wills/Lydden Hill Televised Rallycross Series 1970–1

Champion	Hugh Wheldon	63 points	Mini Cooper
2nd	Tony Skelton	36 points	Mini Cooper
3rd	Brian Chatfield	32 points	Mini Cooper
4th	Jeff Williamson	32 points	Mini Cooper

Embassy Ladies' Invitation Trophy

Champion	Gillian Fortescue-Thomas
2nd	Rosemary Smith
3rd	Jenny Birrell
4th	Bronwyn Burrell

(All girls drove Ford Escort Mexico 1600s supplied by Ford Motor Company)

Non-Televised Sunday Meetings for Wills Embassy Rallycross Trophy

Champion	Hugh Wheldon	56 points	Mini Cooper
2nd	Brian Chatfield	36 points	Mini Cooper
3rd	Gary Streat	31 points	Mini Cooper
4th	Rod Chapman	27 points	Ford Escort

(These were Closed events)

ITV/Castrol/Cadwell Park Televised Rallycross Series 1970–71

Champion	Roger Clark	46 points	Ford 3-litre Capri (4-wheel drive)
2nd	Rod Chapman	42 points	Ford 3-litre Capri (4-wheel drive)

3rd	Stan Clark	25 points	Ford 3-litre Capri (4-wheel drive)
4th	Jeff Williamson	20 points	BL Mini Cooper

Non-Televised Meetings

29th November	1. Paul Hurley	Mini Cooper
	2. John Taylor	Ford Escort
	3. Ian Carroll	Mini Cooper
	4. Philip Walker	Mini Cooper
20th December	1. Jeff Williamson	Mini Cooper
	2. Gerald Braithwaite	Mini Cooper
	3. Stewart Brown	Mini Cooper
	4. John Boulden	Mini Cooper

Guards Rallycross Championship 1970/71 at Croft Autodrome
Non-Televised

Works and Works Sponsored Drivers

1.	John Taylor	50	points	Ford Escort
2.	Rod Chapman	40	points	Ford Escort
3.	Dave Preece	20	points	Mini Cooper
	Ron Charlton	20	points	Anglia

Clubmen

1.	Mike Lawson	45½	points	Mini Cooper
2.	Rod Harrison	23	points	Mini Cooper
	Chris Fishwick	23	points	Mini Cooper
3.	Gerald Braithwaite	18	points	Mini Cooper
4.	Nicky Porter	15	points	Mini Cooper

Appendix 2

RAC RECOGNISED CLUBS ORGANISING AUTOCROSS EVENTS AS LISTED IN THE 1970/71 BLUE BOOK

Aberdare M C
APOC M C (London Counties)
Ashford (Kent) M C
Aberdeen D M C
Abergavenny A C

Burnham on Sea M C
BARC – North West
       North Thames
       East Midlands
       South East
       South West
Bolton le Moors C C
Bewdley A C
Borough 19 M C, Bexley Heath
Buckingham & Dist. M C
Bath M C
Billericay M C
Blackpalfrey M C
Bridgend A C
Bristol M C
Belfast, Bangor M C
Bournemouth M C
Basingstoke C C
Bedford M C
Brighton & Hove M C
Brecon M C

Berwick & Dist. M C
Brent Vale M C (Hayes)
Bruern M C
Bala & Dist. M C, Merioneth
BTRDA

Chester M C
Cheltenham M C
Caithness C C
Cheshunt M C
Canterbury & Dist. C C
Coalville C C
Croydon & Dist. M C
Cambridge C C
Cosmopolitan C C, Portsmouth
Cirencester C C
Cumberland Sporting C C
Chelmsford M C
Central Sussex M C
Chess Valley M C
Coltness C C, Wishaw
Camel Vale M C, Cornwall
Circle C C, Pinner
Coventry M C
Chesterfield & Dist. M C
Craven M C, Camberley

Cemian M C,
Walton-on-Thames
Caern's & Anglesey M C

De Lacy M C, Pontefract
Didcot M C
Dukeries M C
Dungannon M C
Dereham & Dist. C C
Dunsmore M C
Dudley & Dist C C

EMCOS, Gloucester
East Ayrshire C C
East Surrey M C
Exeter M C
Eastbourne & Dist M C
East Anglian M C
Eng. Elec. M C, Rugby
Eastern Counties M C
EMI M C, North Harrow
Exmoor M C

Folkestone C C
Fort Halstead M C
Four Ways C C, Hornchurch
Falcon M C,
South East Midlands
Federation of British Police M C
Farnborough & Dist. M C
Ford Motor Club
Fraserburgh & Dist. M C
55 C C, Perth

Gaynes C C, Hornchurch
Glossop & Dist. C C
Guildford M C
Garstang & Dist. M C

Highland C C, Inverness
Hagley & Dist. C C
Hastings & St Leonards C C

Hawick & Border C C
Herefordshire M C
Haldon M C, Torquay
Holsworthy & Dist. M C
Hartlepool & Dist. M C
High Moor M C
Herbert Ingersol M C
Huddersfield M C
Howden & Dist. M C

Invaders M C, Reading

Jamaica M C

Kentish Border C C
Kirkby Lonsdale C C
Knutsford & Dist. M C
Kings Lynn & Dist. M C
Knowdale C C

Longton & Dist. M C, Preston
Lagos M C
Lion A C, Wales
Liverpool M C
Lancs. & Cheshire C C
Lincoln M C & C C
Larne M C
Lanarkshire C C
Ludlow Castle M C
London M C, Northants
Loughborough C C
Lothian C C
Leicestershire C C

MASSAC, Manchester
Manx A S
Midland Manor M C
Morecambe C C
Mini 7C (North West)
(Midlands)
Mid-Cheshire M R C

153

Maidstone & Mid-Kent M C
MG C C – Abingdon
    Midlands
    North West
    South West
    Scotland
Mid-Antrim M C
Mid-Thames C C

Nuneaton M C
North Humberside M C
North London Enthusiasts C C
North of Ireland M C
Newquay M C
Newcastle & Dist. M C
North Devon M C
Newry & Dist. M C
North Worcestershire A C
North Cornwall
Newtown M C
Northumbrian M C, Durham
North Staffs M C

Orchard M C, Southgate,
            London
Owen Organisation M C
Oxford M C

Peterborough M C
Portsmouth M C
Plymouth M C
Port Talbot M C
Potteries & Newcastle M C

Quinton M C Ltd, Midlands

Rhyl & Dist. M C
Ram M C, Eastbourne
Redditch & Dist. C C
Ross & Dist. M S C
Rochester M C

Rolls-Royce (Derby) M C
Romney Marsh C C
Romford Enthusiasts C C
Rugby M C
Redford & Dist. M C

South East Essex A C
Swansea M C
Southampton M C
South Molton & Dist. M C
Sheffield Students M C
Stranraer C & M C C
Sutton Cheam M C
South Hams M C, South Devon
Sixty-Two C C, Filey
S & WMC, Worcester
Shipley & Dist. M C
West Suffolk M C
South of Scotland M C
Sheffield & Hallamshire M C
Solway C C
Stone Cross A C, Chingford
Southsea M C
Stafford & Dist. C C
Soar Valley M C, Leicester
Solihull (432) M C
Sevenoaks M C
Salisbury & Shaftesbury C C
Scottish Sporting C C Glasgow
Sunderland & Dist. M C
South Bucks. M C
Stockton & Dist. M C
S U N B A C, Birmingham
Sussex C C
Stockport M C
Swindon Phoenix C C
Selby & Dist. M C
Stafford & Dist. C C
Stort Valley A C,
           Sawbridgeworth
Sporting Owner Drivers' Club
Shenstone & Dist. C C

Stonehaven & Dist. M C
South Wales A C, Cardiff
Solway C C
Seven-Fifty M C, Dundee

Trencrom Revellers M C,
                    St Ives
Torbay M C
Taunton M C
Tynemouth & Dist. M C
Truro & Dist. M C
Thames Estuary Automobile
              Club (TEAC)

USSO M C North East
Ulster A C Belfast

USSO M C, North East
Ulster A C, Belfast

Vickers Armstrong (Hurn) M C

Weston-Super-Mare M C
West Essex C C
Welsh Counties C C
Witham & Dist. M C
West Suffolk M C
White Horse M C, Bristol
West Cornwall M C
West Hants & Dorset C C
Worksop & Dist. M C
Welsh Border C C
Worthing M C
Wallasey M C
Whitby & Dist. M C
Winchester & Dist. C C
Woolbridge M C, Dorchester

Yeovil C C
York M C

Names and addresses of club secretaries, for anyone wishing to join a local autocross club, can be obtained from the Royal Automobile Club, Motor Sport Division, 31 Belgrave Square, London SW1.

Index